BECOMING LIGHT

by Erica Jong

Fruits & Vegetables
(poetry, 1971)

Half-Lives
(poetry, 1973)

Fear of Flying
(fiction, 1973)

Loveroot
(poetry, 1975)

How to Save Your Own Life
(fiction, 1977)

At the Edge of the Body
(poetry, 1979)

Fanny: Being the True History of the Adventures of Fanny
Hackabout-Jones
(fiction, 1980)

Witches
(nonfiction, poetry, 1981)

Ordinary Miracles
(poetry, 1983)

Megan's Book of Divorce: A Kid's Book for Adults
(fiction, 1984)

Parachutes & Kisses
(fiction, 1984)

Erica Jong

❖

BECOMING
LIGHT

Poems
New and Selected

Harper Perennial
A Division of HarperCollins*Publishers*

Grateful acknowledgment is made to the publishers for permission to reprint the works listed below.

From *Loveroot* by Erica Jong. Copyright © 1968, 1969, 1973, 1974, 1975 by Erica Mann Jong. Reprinted by permission of Henry Holt and Company, Inc.

To Pablo Neruda

Dear Colette

Dear Marys, Dear Mother, Dear Daughter (originally published as Mary, Mary)

Elegy for a Whale

For My Sister, Against Narrowness

For My Husband

Cheever's People

Dear Anne Sexton, I

Dear Anne Sexton, II

Dearest Man-in-the-Moon

Dear Keats

Becoming a Nun

Empty

Egyptology

Parable of the Four-Poster

Tapestry, with Unicorn

The Poet Writes in *I*

Sunjuice

Insomnia & Poetry

From *How to Save Your Own Life* by Erica Jong. Copyright © 1977 by Erica Mann Jong. Reprinted by permission of Henry Holt and Company, Inc.

The Puzzle

The Long Tunnel of Wanting You

The Muse Who Came to Stay

We Learned

Doubts Before Dreaming

The Dirty Laundry Poem

Sailing Home

Living Happily Ever After

The Surgery of the Sea

After the Earthquake

From *Witches* by Erica Jong. Copyright © 1981 by Erica Mann Jong. Reprinted by permission of Harry N. Abrams, Inc.

To the Goddess

To the Horned God

Figure of the Witch

Baby-Witch

How to Name Your Familiar

Her Broom, or the Ride of the Witch

Love Magick

Bitter Herb

For All Those Who Died

A Deadly Herbal in Verse (Mandrake, Henbane, Thorn Apple, Deadly Nightshade, Monkshood)

A hardcover edition of this book was published in 1991 by HarperCollins Publishers.

BECOMING LIGHT: POEMS NEW AND SELECTED. Copyright © 1961, 1962, 1971, 1973, 1975, 1977, 1979, 1981, 1983, 1987, 1991 by Erica Mann Jong. All rights reserved. Printed in the United States of America. No part of this book may be used or reproduced in any manner whatsoever without written permission except in the case of brief quotations embodied in critical articles and reviews. For information address HarperCollins Publishers, Inc., 10 East 53rd Street, New York, NY 10022.

HarperCollins books may be purchased for educational, business, or sales promotional use. For information please write: Special Markets Department, HarperCollins Publishers, Inc., 10 East 53rd Street, New York, NY 10022.

Designed by Irving Perkins Associates

The Library of Congress has catalogued the hardcover edition as follows:

Jong, Erica.
    Becoming light : poems new and selected / Erica Jong.—1st ed.
    p.   cm.
    ISBN 0-06-018316-0
    1. Title.
    PS3560.O56B43   1991   91-55101
    811'.54—dc20

ISBN 0-06-098420-1 (pbk.)

03 02 01 00   RRD(H)   10   9   8

To
K.D.B.
keeper of my flame

*Time is what keeps the light
from reaching us.*
          —Meister Eckhart

seven lives,
then we
become light . . .

Contents

I New Poems *Lullabye for a Dybbuk*

II   Early Poems

III   From *Fruits & Vegetables* (1971)

IV   From *Half-Lives* (1973)

V From *Loveroot* (1975)

VI From *How to Save Your Own Life* (1977)

IX   From *Ordinary Miracles* (1983)

Preface

It was in honor of the birthday of Edward Lear that an editor at the *New York Times Magazine* asked me to write something commemorating the versifier who perfected the smile in the sneer known as a limerick. I wrote a limerick for Edward Lear and then this "Epitaph for Myself."

A demi-young author named Jong
Became famous for reasons quite wrong.
A poet at heart, she won fame as a tart——
That mispronounced poet called Jong.

That fugitive piece of doggerel was my way of dealing with the absurdity of my public persona. I had begun literary life as a poet and poetry was still the most important thing I did——even in a world of prose. My novels and essays were essentially a poet's novels and essays—— besotted with language and filled with my visual and visceral delight in words. Somehow, in a culture where everyone is alloted no more than a thirty-second sound byte, I had become Erica "Zipless Fuck" Jong. But that never meant that *I* bought the package. On the contrary, it was my poetry that kept me sane, that kept me whole, that kept me alive.

Poetry, however, is not easy to midwife into the world. Most publishers don't want it (I will always be grateful to Gladys Justin Carr, William Shinker, and the other true booklovers at HarperCollins for being the exceptions that prove the rule) and most bookstores and review media ignore it. Nevertheless, at the climactic moments of our lives——death of a loved one, heartbreak, new love, the birth of a baby——we turn to poetry, and nothing else will do.

"Poetry is the honey of all flowers; the quintessence of all sciences . . . the marrow of wit . . . the very phrase of angels," said Thomas Nashe,

Shakespeare's contemporary, in 1592. And so it still remains. Every funeral, every wedding, every honeymoon (married or not), every bris or christening is an occasion for poetry—and even in this epoch of sound bytes and MTV, people dig through tattered anthologies to find the fitting words.

Why is this? Because poetry comforts as nothing else can and because, apparently, we are still a race for whom magic is a word. The incantation both propitiates and validates the event. Since flesh can't stay, we pass the words along.

These poems are the few I have chosen to save from my five published volumes of poetry, my second novel which contains a coda in verse, and my book on witches and witchcraft. (It will come as no surprise to my readers that I have been trying to blend genres from the beginning.) There is also a large complement of new poems and a series of early, previously unpublished poems which date back to my teens and twenties. Disowned when I published *Fruits & Vegetables* (in part because they betray my origins as a more formal poet who loved rhyme and meter), I am now ready to own them again. I started life as a poet, and a formal poet at that. It took maturity to let me love Whitman, Dickinson, and Allen Ginsberg. At last I am ready to own both my free and my metered sides.

My deepest thanks to Jay Parini, Gladys Justin Carr, and Tom Miller for helping me edit thirty years of poetry into one manageable volume; to Lavinia Lorch for shaping my English to an Italian cadence (in *Nota in una Bottiglia*); to my parents for reading me poetry when I was little; and to my daughter for loving to have that tradition passed along.

For that is what poetry is: a passing along.

Inevitably, these poems form a sort of autobiography in verse. I hope they are the reader's autobiography as well as the writer's.

Erica Jong
Weston, Connecticut
May 1991

I

❖

NEW POEMS

Lullabye for a Dybbuk

Lullabye for a Dybbuk

The old self
like a dybbuk
clutching at my heel.
She wants to come back.
She is digging
her long red nails
into the tender meat of my thighs . .
She tweaks my clit,
hoping that my sexaholic self
will surface
and take me back, back, back

to the land of fuck,
where, crazed with lust
I come over and over again,
going nowhere.

The old self
does not like
her displacement.
She resents the new tenant
sprucing up
her disorderly house.

She resents
the calm woman
nourishing her roses,
her daughter, her dogs,
her poems, her passionate

friendships.
She wants chaos
and angst and *Liebestod*.
She claims
she can't write
without them.

But the new tenant
is wise to her tricks.
Disorder is not poetry,
she says. *Pain*
is not love.
Love flowers; love gives
without taking;
love is serene
and calm.

I talk to the dybbuk:

My darling dybbuk,
I will love you
into submission.
Tweak me, I will only
caress you.
Claw me, I will only
kiss you back.

For what I have learned
lets me love
even my demon.

Demon——I love you
for you are
mine,
I say.

And demons die
of love.

4

Ode to My Shoes

(After Neruda, who left us his socks)

The poet alone
is writing an ode
to her shoes—
her shoes which
only she can fill,
her shoes of purple suede and green leather
the color of palm fronds,
her diamond-studded boots,
her feathered cowboy boots,
her flame cowboy boots,
her seven-league epic poetry boots,
her little silver haiku boots
with the tiny heels that twinkle,
her first-person platform boots
and her backless glass slippers
modelled after Cinderella's
(one lost, at midnight,
because of a running man),
her huntress boots of India-rubber,
her lover's boots joined at the ankle
like leg irons,
her pink baby booties bronzed
for posterity,
her daughter's burning Reeboks,
her lover's laceless sneakers

5

left in the guest room closet
for her to kiss
year after year
after year.

Darling shoes,
beloved feet,
ten toes to walk me
toward my true love,
fuck-me pumps to fuel his passion,
stiletto heels to stab him
if he strays.

Shoes tell you everything.
Shoes speak my language.
Their tap tap tap on the airport runway
tells me the story
of a lovely, lonely woman flying after love—
that old, old story
in a new pair
of shoes.

Alphabet Poem: To the Letter I

I, io, ich, yo, Я,
uppercase, lowercase,
sometimes confused with love
which starts with L,
but could easily be I,
with a foot,
a pseudopod facing the future,
or at least the righthand
margin of the page—
all we know of life
and all we need
to know.

The poet must abolish I,
said Keats;
have no identity,
be as water flowing
around a rock—
a voice for all
the unsaid waves within,
antenna of the deep.

"Here lies one whose name
was writ in water,"
he would have graven
on his gravestone
had he but world enough
and time—

but the harpstring broke,
and his dearest friends
would not deny his I—
(they could not
for they still believed
themselves).

Ich, I, io, yo, Я
turned from *lettres majuscules*
to minuscule
by cummings
(ee, I mean)

to droplets of vapor
condensed along a blade
of grass
(by Whitman),
to Blake's tiger,
to Dickinson's
buzzing fly . . .
(we so insist
on having names,
then die).

For the poet
whoever he (or she)
may be
is always
beneath the violets
singing like wind
or water.

To become a natural thing,
eye of the cosmos,
sans i's, sans teeth,
sans everything,
to see the rock,
the hand, the water,
rippling around

8

the thrown pebble
as part of the same art,
the art of the possible,
life passing into death
and death to life—
poetry not politics.

The abolition of the I,
eye, eye,
the end of i,
so that even the dot
becomes a flyspeck,
Morse code
of infinity . . .

The alphabet is
poetry's DNA;
what sperm and egg

are to our progeny,
the alphabet
is to the poet,
germ-cells,
single, yet dividing
like a zygote,
characters
encompassing
the world.

We are all one poet
and always
we have one
communal name,
god's name, nameless,
a flame in the heart,
a breath,
a gust of air,
prana whistling in the dark.

i dies—
but the breath
lingers on
through the medium
of the magic
alphabet
and in its wake
death is no more
than metaphor.

Demeter at Dusk

At dusk Demeter
        becomes afraid
        for baby Persephone
        lost in that hell
   which she herself created
with her love.

Excess of love—
the woman's curse,
the curse of loving
that which causes pain,
the curse of bringing forth
in pain,
the curse of bearing,
bearing always pain.

Demeter pauses, listening for her child—
this fertile goddess
with her golden hair, bringing forth
wheat and fruit and wildflowers
knee-high.
This apple-breasted goddess
whose sad eyes
will bless the frozen world,
bring spring again—
all because she once
walked through the night
and loved a man, half-demon,

angel-tongued,
who gave her
everything she needed to be wise:
a daughter,
hell's black night,
then endless
    spring.

The Impressionists

They conspired to paint the air
knowing that art
is not only a way
of seeing
but a way
of being,
a passion for the light,
a tenderness at heart
just short
of being wounded by the air,
a toughness too.

They conspired to paint the air,
to anatomize each light mote,
to imprism each speck of dust
until the air danced with color
and every inhaled breath
became a rainbow in the lungs.

Jasmine, tea leaf, camellia,
tuberose and thyme—the air
turning to color, the color
bleeding into earth, the
earth giving forth its forms,
its fossils, its sexual smells,
then closing over all.

They conspired to paint the air,
leaving their mark,

an obsessed life,
infinitely rich,
infinitely ripe,
tasting of peaches
and anemones,
red tile,
voile peignoirs
and air,
inhabited air.

To My Brother Poet, Seeking Peace

People wish to be settled. Only as long as they are unsettled is there any hope for them.

—Thoreau

My life has been
the instrument
for a mouth
I have never seen,
breathing wind
which comes
from I know not
where,
arranging and changing
my moods,
so as to make
an opening
for his voice.

Or hers.
Muse, White Goddess
mother with invisible
milk,
androgynous god
in whose grip
I struggle,
turning this way and that,

15

believing that I chart
my life,
my loves,
when in fact
it is she, he,
who charts them—
all for the sake
of some
as yet unwritten poem.

Twisting in the wind,
twisting like a pirate
dangling in a cage
from a high seawall,
the wind whips
through my bones
making an instrument,
my back a xylophone,
my sex a triangle
chiming,
my lips stretched tight
as drumskins,

I no longer care
who is playing me,
but fear
makes the hairs
stand up
on the backs
of my hands
when I think
that she may stop.

And yet I long
for peace
as fervently as you do—
the sweet connubial bliss

that admits no
turbulence,
the settled life
that defeats poetry,
the hearth before which
children play—
not poets' children,
ragtag, neurotic, demon-ridden,
but the apple-cheeked children
of the bourgeoisie.

My daughter dreams
of peace
as I do:
marriage, proper house,
proper husband,
nourishing dreamless
sex,
love like a hot toddy,
or an apple pie.

But the muse
has other plans
for me
and you.

Puppet mistress,
dangling us
on this dark proscenium,
pulling our strings,
blowing us
toward Cornwall,
toward Venice, toward Delphi,
toward some lurching
counterpane,
a tent upheld
by one throbbing

blood-drenched pole—
her pen, her pencil,
the monolith
we worship,
underneath
the gleaming moon.

My Daughter Says

My daughter says
she feels like a Martian,
that no one understands her,
that one friend is too perfect,
and another too mean,
and that she has
the earliest bedtime
in her whole class.

I strain to remember
how a third grader feels
about love, about pain
and I feel a hollow in my heart
where there should be blood
and an ache where there should
be certainty.

My darling Molly,
no earthling ever lived
who did not feel
like a Martian,
who did not curse her bedtime,
who did not wonder
how she got to this planet,
who dropped her here
and why
and how she can possibly
stay.

I go to bed
whenever I like
and with whomever I choose,
but still I wonder
why I do not
belong in my class,
and where my class is anyway,
and why so many of them
seem to be asleep
while I toss and turn
in perplexity.

They, meanwhile, imagine I am perfect
and have solved everything:
an earthling among the Martians,
at home on her home planet,
feet planted in green grass.

If only we could all admit
that none of us belongs here,
that all of us are Martians,
and that our bedtimes
are always
too early
or

too late.

Driving Me Away

Driving me away
is easier
than saying
goodbye—

kissing the air,
the last syllable
of truth
being always
two lips compressed
around
emptiness—

the emptiness
you dread
yet return to
as just punishment,
just reward.

Who
loved you
so relentlessly?
Who lost you
in that howling void
between infancy
and death?

It is punctuated
by the warm bodies
of women,
who hold you for a while
then run
down that echoing corridor,
doing
as they are told.

The Land of Fuck

Here I was begging the Muse not to get
me in trouble with the powers that be, not
to make me write out all those "filthy"
words . . . pointing out in that deaf and
dumb language which I employed when
dealing with the Voice that soon I
would have to write my books in jail or at
the foot of the gallows . . . and these holy
cows deep in clover render a verdict of
guilty, guilty of dreaming it up "to make
money"!

—Henry Miller

The land of fuck
is not for sale.

Caught between
the muslin curtains
of the nursery
and the red damask
of the whorehouse,
the gambling den,
the mafia chieftains'
restaurant
(in whose backroom the big men
with big bellies,
big guns,
and little dicks

gamble lives
away
on a flipped card
or a throw
of bones)—

the land of fuck
is not for sale.

You can steal it
if you dare.

In a dream
you can ascend
to that special room
above the shadowy El
where, amid the rattling trains
carrying bug-eyed
exhibitionists
and drooling
adolescent boys
with perpetual
hard-ons,
the students of Fuck
go to spill their lives away
and the semen pools
under their luminous chairs.

The land of fuck
is not for sale
any more than
the sea is,
and it smells the same.

Ocean wreckage
at low tide: salt and rot
and sea meat left in the sun
too long,

sweet slime
between epochs of bone
and dust.
The land of fuck
is not for sale—
which does not mean
it has no price.

The tax
is tranquility, calm,
and the stillness of life.

The land of fuck
has a price.

Middle Aged Lovers, I

Unable to bear
the uncertainty
of the future,
we consulted seers,
mediums, stock market gurus,
psychics who promised
happiness on this
or another planet,
astrologists of love,
seekers of the Holy Grail.

Looking for certainty
we asked for promises,
lover's knots, pledges, rings,
certificates, deeds of ownership,
when it was always enough
to let your hand
pass over my body,
your eyes find the depths of my own,
and the wind pass over our faces
as it will pass
through our bones,
sooner than we think.

The current is love,
is poetry,
the blood beat
in the thighs,

the electrical charge
in the brain.

Our long leap
into the unknown
began nearly
a half century ago
and is almost
over.

I think of the
amphorae of stored honey
at Paestum
far out-lasting
their Grecian eaters,
or of the furniture
in a pharaoh's tomb
on which
no one sits.

Trust the wind,
my lover,
and the water.

They have the
answers
to all your questions

and mine.

The Rain Is My Home

All my life
I have resented
umbrellas:
middle child
defying the rain,
seeing rainbows
in the parachutes of grey
that collapse over our heads
on rainy days,

I skip in the shiny streets
hearing the songs in the tires,
and loving the sound
of the rain.

Long before I surrendered
to my fate,
I surrendered
to the rain—
a fugue by Bach
raining softly on my head
teaching me fearlessness.

Reader: I give you
this rain.

The Raspberries in My Driveway

*Nature will bear the closest inspection. She
invites us to lay our eyes level with her
smallest leaf, and take an insect view of its
plain.*

—Thoreau

The raspberries
in my driveway
have always
been here
(for the whole eleven years
I have owned
but have not owned
this house),
yet
I have never
tasted them
before.

Always on a plane.
Always in the arms
of man, not God,
always too busy,
too fretful,
too worried
to see
that all along

my driveway
are red, red raspberries
for me to taste.

Shiny and red,
without hairs—
unlike the berries
from the market.
Little jewels—
I share them
with the birds!

On one perches
a tiny green insect.
I blow her off.
She flies!
I burst the raspberry
upon my tongue.

In my solitude
I commune
with raspberries,
with grasses,
with the world.

The world was always
there before,
but where
was *I?*

Ah raspberry—
if you are so beautiful
upon my ready tongue,
imagine
what wonders
lie in store
for me!

In the Glass-Bottomed Boat

In the glass-bottomed boat
of our lives, we putter along
gazing at that other world
under the sea—
that world of flickering
yellow-tailed fish,
of deadly moray eels, of sea urchins
like black stars
that devastate great brains
of coral,
of fish the color
of blue neon,
& fish the color
of liquid silver
made by Indians
exterminated
centuries ago.

We pass, we pass,
always looking down.
The fish do not
look up at us,
as if they knew
somehow
their world
for the eternal one,
ours for
the merely time-bound.

The engine sputters.
Our guide—a sweet
black boy with skin
the color of molten chocolate—
asks us of the price of jeans
& karate classes
in the States.
Surfboards too
delight him—
& skateboards.
He wants to sail, sail, sail,
not putter
through the world.

& so do we,
so do we,
wishing for the freedom
of the fish
beneath the reef,
wishing for the crevices
of sunken ship
with its rusted eyeholes,
its great ribbed hull,
its rotted rudder,
its bright propeller
tarnishing beneath the sea.

"They sunk this ship
on purpose,"
says our guide—
which does not surprise
us,
knowing how life
always imitates
even the shabbiest
art.
Our brains forged
in shark & seawreck epics,

we fully expect to see
a wreck like this one,
made on purpose
for our eyes.

But the fish swim on,
intimating death,
intimating outer space,
& even the oceans
within the body
from which we come.

The fish are uninterested
in us.
What hubris to think
a shark concentrates
as much on us
as we on him!

The creatures of the reef
spell death, spell life,
spell eternity,
& still we putter on
in our leaky little boat,
halfway there,
halfway there.

Pane Caldo

Rising in the morning
like warm bread,
from a bed
in America,
the aroma
of my baking
reaches you
in Italy,
rocking in your boat
near the Ponte Longo,
cutting through the glitter
of yesterday's moonlight
on your sunstruck
canal.

My delicious baker—
it is you
who have made
this hot bread
rise.
It is you
who have split the loaf
and covered it with the butter.

I prayed to the moon
streaking the still lagoon
with her skyblue manna;
I prayed for you

to sail into my life,
parting the waters,
making them whole.

And here you come,
half captain, half baker—

& the warm aroma of bread
crosses
the ocean
we share.

Nota in una Bottiglia

Mandando una lettera
da New York a Venezia
da amante ad amante,
da Inglese Americano
ad Italiano Veneziano,
e come mandare
una nota in una bottiglia
da un mare
ad un altro,
da una galassia
ad un altra,
da un epoca
ad un altra,
scirolando per creppacci
nello spazio.

Mio amante
così lontano
eppure qui
dentro alla mia anima,
quando respiri
al telefono,
un canale
si apre
nel mio cuore,
un canale chiaro
in quel mondo scintillante,
dove ci cullavamo
in una barca

amandoci,
sapendoci parte
della danza
del mare.

E tutt' uno.
La barca
abbracciata dall' acqua
e i corpi nostri
abbracciati l'uno
all' altro,
e la luce del sole
strisciando il mare
finchè il plenilunio
lo colma,
e nel tondo della luna
nasce il nostro amore.

L'amore ci guarisce
perchè ci ricorda
l'integrità
che abbiamo perso
nella nostra lotta
contro noi stessi.

E in questa bottiglia
ti mando quella integrità
e il mare la solleva
e la lascia cader
giù.

La luna e la nostra postina
Porterà il messaggio.
Io aspetto sulla spiaggia
il suo sorgere.
Rendo questo scintillio
nelle sue mani
capaci.

To a Transatlantic Mirror

*When we become truly ourselves, we just
become a swinging door . . .*

—Suzuki

Sick of the self,
the self-seducing self—
with its games, its fears,
its misty memories, and its prix fixe menu
of seductions (so familiar
even to the seducer)
that he grows sick
of looking at himself
in the mirrored ceiling
before he takes the plunge into this new
distraction from the self
which in fact leads back
to self.

Self—the prison.
Love—the answer and the door.
And yet the self should also be a door,
swinging, letting loves both in and out,
for change
is the world's only fixity, and fixity
her foremost lie.

How to trust love
which has so often

betrayed the betrayer,
seduced the seducer,
and then turned out
to be not even love?
We are jaded,
divorced from our selves
without ever having found
ourselves——and yet we
long for wholeness
if not fixity,
for harmony
if not music of the spheres.

If life is a flood
and there is no ark,
then where do the animals float
two by two?

I refuse to believe
that the flesh falls
from their bones
without understanding
ever coming,
and I refuse to believe
that we must leave
this life entirely alone.

Much harumphing
across the ocean,
my brother poet coughs,
clears his throat
(he smokes too much),
and gazes into the murky
depths of his word-processor,
as if it were a crystal ball.
I do not know
all that hides
in his heart of darkness
but I know I love

the thoughts
that cloud the surface
of his crystal ball.

He longs to leap
headlong into his future
and cannot.
This chapter's finished,
his self peels back
a skin.
Snakes hiss,
shedding their scales.
The goddess smiles.
She sends her missives
only to the brave.

Middle Aged Lovers, II

You open to me
a little,
then grow afraid
and close again,
a small boy
fearing to be hurt,
a toe stubbed
in the dark,
a finger cut
on paper.

I think I am free
of fears,
enraptured, abandoned
to the call
of the Bacchae,
my own siren,
tied to my own
mast,
both Circe
and her swine.

But I too
am afraid:
I know where
life leads.

The impulse
to join,

to confess all,
is followed
by the impulse
to renounce,

and love—
imperishable love—
must die,
in order
to be reborn.

We come
to each other
tentatively,
veterans of other
wars,
divorce warrants
in our hands
which we would beat
into blossoms.

But blossoms
will not withstand
our beatings.

We come
to each other
with hope
in our hands—
the very thing
Pandora kept
in her casket
when all the ills
and woes of the world
escaped.

Gazing Out, Gazing In

(to my lover gazing out the window)

Because I am here
anchoring you
to the passionate darkness,
you gaze out the window
at the light.

My love is the thing
that frees you
to follow your eyes,

as your love,
a sword made of moonlight
and blood,
and smelling of sex
and salt marshes,
frees me to gaze
with a calm inward
eye.

In all your frenzied searching
you never stood
calmly at the window.

But now the sea,
the city and the sky

are all seen
as if from a perch
at the edge of the cosmos,
where I sit behind you
gazing
at the fire.

The Demon Lover

Unable to bear the falsehoods—
the girls calling up
each time you came
to my bed—
I fled
and now I dream of you

knowing you are
dreaming of me,
knowing we will always be
each other's muse, forbidden lover,
witch and warlock
joined by a filament of flesh,
lover through the looking glass.

I dream of you
as the witch
beside her husband's hearth
dreams of the grandmaster
of the coven,
dreams of burning stones
that sting the flesh,
while her good husband
strokes her rump,
muttering words
of tame domestic love.

You are my demon,
the devil in my flesh,

the wild child,
the boy with eyes of flame,
the bad seed I took
into my body,
the infected needle
I craved
more deeply
than health.

On every seashore
I see you waving your arms
out of the whitecaps
as you drown
only to be reborn
in the foam
between my legs.

In every bed
you appear, sexual dybbuk,
mocking my lovers
with your twinkling blue eyes
and the crooked cane of your cock
smelling of the pit.

You are trouble, double trouble,
triple trouble,
the wrecker of peace,
but you make
my cauldron boil.

I dream of you always
as I lie
in the sheltering arms
of another.
I dream of you
as the condemned witch
dreams of her end
at the stake,

when, lashed to the burning pole,
she will offer up her flesh
to become smoke,
her hair to become ash,
her soul to be carried away
on the wings of the air,
marrying, marrying, marrying
the final fire.

In My Cauldron Under the Full Moon

In my cauldron
under the full moon
thinking of poppets:
who shall I choose
to join
my life with?

The man of muslin
with the peppermint
heart, bleeding
through his pocket
underneath
the felt-tipped pens?

The man of plastic
listening to jazz
in his blue room?

The sexual robot
with his swiveling
indefatigable cock?

The yearning poet
who would rather yearn
than anything?

The businessman
who thinks poetry
has a bottom line?

The absent daddy
who will only come home
when the flesh
is falling off his bones?

I would
make a poppet, Muse,
but I do not know
how to mark it.

Which astrological sign,
which profession,
which color of hair,
which size and shape of cock?

Witch-woman that I am,
I am baffled
by choices.

Therefore I turn it over
to you,
and your lunar wisdom,
while I wait
in my cauldron
bubbling
under a pregnant
moon.

I Sit at My Desk Alone

I sit at my desk alone
as I did on many Sunday
afternoons when you came
back to me,
your arms aching for me,
though they smelled
of other women
and your sweet head bowed
for me to rub
and your heart bursting
with things to tell me,
and your hair
and your eyes
wild.

We would embrace
on the carpet
and leave
the imprint of our bodies
on the floor.
My back is still sore
where you pressed me
into the rug,
a sweet soreness I would never
lose.

I think of you always
on Sunday afternoons,
and I try to conjure you
with these words—

as if you might
come back to me
at twilight—
but you are never coming back—
never.

The truth is
you no longer exist.
Oh you walk the world
sturdily enough:
one foot in front
of the other.
But the lover you were,
the tender shoot
springing within me,
trusting me with your dreams,
has hardened
into fear and cynicism.

Betrayal does that—
betrays the betrayer.

I want to hate you
and I cannot.
But I cannot
love you either.

It is our old love
I love,
as one loves
certain images
from childhood—
shards
shining in
the street
in the shit.

Shards of light
in the darkness.

Love Spell: Against Endings

All the endings in my life
rise up against me
like that sea of troubles
Shakespeare mixed
with metaphors;
like Vikings in their boats
singing Wagner,
like witches
burning at
the stake——
I submit
to my fate.

I know beginnings,
their sweetnesses,
and endings,
their bitternesses——
but I do not know
continuance——
I do not know
the sweet demi-boredom
of life as it lingers,
of man and wife
regarding each other
across a table of shared witnesses,
of the hand-in-hand dreams
of those who have slept

a half-century together
in a bed so used and familiar
it is rutted
with love.

I would know that
before this life closes,
a soulmate to share my roses—
I would make a spell
with long grey beard hairs
and powdered rosemary and rue,
with the jacket of a tux
for a tall man
with broad shoulders,
who loves to dance;
with one blue contact lens
for his bluest eyes;
with honey in a jar
for his love of me;
with salt in a dish
for his love of sex and skin;
with crushed rose petals
for our bed;
with tubes of cerulean blue
and vermilion and rose madder
for his artist's-eye;
with a dented Land-Rover fender
for his love of travel;
with a poem by Blake
for his love of innocence
revealed by experience;
with soft rain
and a bare head;
with hand-in-hand dreams on Mondays
and the land of fuck
on Sundays;
with mangoes, papayas

and limes,
and a house towering
above the sea.

Muse, I surrender
to thee.
Thy will be done,
not mine.

If this love spell
pleases you,
send me this lover,
this husband,
this dancing partner
for my empty bed
and let him fill me
from now
until I die.

I offer my bones,
my poems,
my luck with roses,
and the secret garden
I have found
walled in my center,
and the sunflower
who raises her head
despite her heavy seeds.

I am ready now, Muse,
to serve you faithfully
even with
a graceful dancing partner—
for I have learned
to stand alone.

Give me your blessing.
Let the next

epithalamion I write
be my own.
And let it last
more than the years
of my life—
and without the least
strain—
two lovers bareheaded
in a summer rain.

Beast, Book, Body

I was sick of being a woman,
sick of the pain,
the irrelevant detail of sex,
my own concavity
uselessly hungering
and emptier whenever it was filled,
and filled finally
by its own emptiness,
seeking the garden of solitude
instead of men.

The white bed
in the green garden—
I looked forward
to sleeping alone
the way some long
for a lover.

Even when you arrived,
I tried to beat you
away with my sadness,
my cynical seductions,
and my trick of
turning a slave
into a master.

And all because
you made

my fingertips ache
and my eyes cross
in passion
that did not know its own name.

Bear, beast, lover
of the book of my body,
you turned my pages
and discovered
what was there
to be written
on the other side.

And now
I am blank
for you,
a *tabula rasa*
ready to be printed
with letters
in an undiscovered language
by the great press
of our love.

The Whole Point

—Vermont, August 5, 1989
Erica to Ken

The red and black biplane
swoops down
on the green hills
of Vermont.

A little airstrip
between two mountain ranges,
and people coming
with balloons and streamers,
kites, gliders
and winged wishes.

The bride climbs out
trailing wildflowers,
parachutes, kisses,

and the groom, big beast
with soft eyes that gleam
like butter,
grins, a horny boyscout,
and scoops her
in his arms.

*Fearful, I have walked this world
not daring to hope*

for the cut half
severed from me
in my last life.

Defiant, I have flown
above my fears, flaunted them
like you, scattering jokes
to drown the sound
of my heart cracking
like winter ice,
and to still
the heckling
of the gallery.

And now you come
to tell me
you know the child
behind the wanton smile
and that you love her
as I know the boy
inside the rough beast
and I can lead him
home.

They marry in a field
of wildflowers
near a pond
whose least ripple
betrays the spirit within.

Intermediate
between earth and sky,
this palimpsest
for the mind of God
has caught the clouds
within its brimming bowl.

Butterflies and hummingbirds
hover nearby.

Deer tiptoe unafraid
on delicate hooves,
and crickets and bullfrogs
chorus.

The red and black biplane
takes off,
banks, turns and flies through
a green notch
in the mountains.
It soars into the blue,
seeming to disappear
into a cloud.

In a little while
it will come back to earth.

Perhaps that is the whole point.

The Color of Snow

For David Karetsky (April 14, 1940–
March 12, 1991), killed in an
avalanche

Putting the skis down
in the white snow,
the wind singing,
the blizzard of time
going past your eyes,

it is a little
like being snowed in
in the Connecticut house
on a day when the world
goes away

and only the white dog
follows you out
to make fresh tracks
in the long blue shadow
of the mountain.

We are all halfway there,
preferring not
to think about it.
You went down the mountain
first,
in a blaze of light,

reminding us
to seize our lives,
to live with the wind
whistling in our ears,
and the light bedazzling
the tips of our skis

and the people we love
waiting in the lodge below
scribbling lines
on paper the color
of snow,

knowing there is no
holding on
but only the wind singing
and these lines of light
shining
in the fresh snow.

The Bed of the World

The great bed of the world
arching over graves
over Babi Yar
with its multitudes of bones,
with battallions of screams
frozen in a concrete glacier,
with pillows of earth
and comforters of green grass
covering all that dead flesh.

Dead flesh shall live again—
a dream in god's endless night—
rise green out of the earth
as grass, as trees, as tomato stalks
bearing a bright red fruit
and the feuds of man- and womankind
shall be fed again from the same seeds:
the tomato, the mythic pomegranate, the biblical apple
all rising from the grass that springs
out of the screams of stopped mouths.

Sometimes I dream
that my bed is built over a ravine,
the ravine of Babi Yar, any ravine
where thousands died
and I moan in pleasure to propitiate the earth,
to make fruit ripen
and trees wave green leaves like banners
all because love can touch me still.

It is never enough to create.
The beast must feed its meat teeth too.
Out of the screaming mouth of earth
we feed the grass that covers
all our beds.

I wish I did not know all that I know.
Galaxies spin, grass grows, and people kill.
We are the only race to murder for our dreams—
and not for hunger,
hungering for dreams.

II

❖

EARLY POEMS

Venice, November, 1966

With his head full of Shakespearean tempests
and old notions of poetic justice,
he was ready with his elegies
the day the ocean sailed into the square.

"The sea," he wrote, "is a forgiving element,
and history only the old odor of blood.
She will come to rest on the soft floor
of the world, barnacled like a great pirate ship,
and blind fish—mouthing like girls before a glass—
will bump, perhaps, San Marco's brittle bones."

Pleased with these images, he paused
and conjured visions of a wet apocalypse:
the blown church bobbing like a monstrous water toy,
Doge Dandolo's bronze horses from Byzantium
pawing the black waves, incredulous pigeons
hovering like gulls over the drowning square,
mosaic saints floating gently to pieces.

Then he waited as the wind rose, as gondoliers
were rocking in the long furrows of their boats
and small waves licked the marble lions' eyes.
But still this most improbable of cities
hung on, lewdly enjoying her own smell.

Learning later how Florence, with her brown bells,
her dried-up joke of a river, had played

the ark to all his fantasies of flood,
he felt a little foolish. He was walking
in the gallery then, thinking of the doges:
how they tread on clouds which puff and pucker
like the flesh of their fat Venetian whores;
how thanks to Tintoretto's shrewd, old eyes,
they saw themselves amid the holy saints;
how shrewd, old Tintoretto, for a price,
painted his patrons into paradise.

For an Earth-Landing

the sky sinks its blue teeth
into the mountains.

Rising on pure will

(the lurch & lift-off,
the sudden swing
into wide, white snow),

I encourage the cable.

Past the wind
& crossed tips of my skis
& the mauve shadows of pines
& the spoor of bears
& deer,

I speak to my fear,

rising, riding,
finding myself

the only thing
between snow & sky,

the link
that holds it all together.

Halfway up the wire,
we stop,
slide back a little
(a whirr of pulleys).

Astronauts circle above us today
in the television blue of space.

But the thin withers of alps
are waiting to take us too,
& this might be the moon!

We move!

Friends, this is a toy
merely for reaching mountains

merely
for skiing down.

& now we're dangling
like charms on the same bracelet

or upsidedown tightrope people
(a colossal circus!)

or absurd winged walkers,
angels in animal fur,

with mittened hands waving
& fear turning

& the mountain,
like a fisherman,

reeling us all in.

So we land
on the windy peak,
touch skis to snow,
are married to our purple shadows,
& ski back down
to the unimaginable valley

leaving no footprints.

Still Life with Tulips

Because you did, I too arrange flowers,
Watching the pistils jut like insolent tongues
And the hard, red flesh of the petals
Widening beneath my eyes. They move like the hands
Of clocks, seeming not to move except
When I turn my gaze; then savagely
In the white room, they billow and spread
Until their redness engulfs me utterly.

Mother, you are far away and claim
In mournful letters that I do not need you;
Yet here in this sunny room, your tulips
Devour me, sucking hungrily
My watery nourishment, filling my house
Like a presence, like an enemy.

Geared to your intervals as the small hand
Of a clock repeats the larger, I,
Your too-faithful daughter, still drag behind you,
Turning in the same slow circles.

Across the years and distances, my hands
Among these fierce, red blossoms repeat
Your gestures. I hope my daughter never writes:
"Because you did, I too arrange flowers."

Ritratto

He was a two-bit Petrarchist who lounged
Near the Uffizi in the ochre afternoons
Surveying the girls. A certain insolence
In how he moved his hips, his stony eyes,
His hands which seemed to cup their breasts like fruit
As they slid by, pretending blank disdain,
Won him a modest reputation in a place
Where sad-eyed satyrs of an ageless middle age
Are seldom scarce.
                          On rainy days he stalked
The galleries. Between the Giottos
And Masaccios, he slithered hissing
In his moccasins, and whistling low.

His metaphors were old; the girls were young.
Their eyes (he said) were little lakes of blue
(Rolling the *bella lingua* off his tongue).
Their hair was gold, their lips like flowers that grew
Within his *bel' giardino* on the hill.
(Although he had no garden on the hill,
In summer the young girls grew thick as weeds.)

Blonds were his passion but (like Tacitus) he thought
The German fräuleins blowzy, rugged, rough
And yet inevitable: August brought
Such hordes as might have sacked another Rome.
He always sent the fair barbarians home
With something Burckhardt hardly hinted at.
(He kept his assignations in a Fiat.)

You should have seen his little pied-à-terre——
Two blocks from where his mother lived; there
He kept his treasures: blonds of every nation——
(Two dozen half-undressed U.N. legations)——
Were photographically ensconced along his wall.
Beside the crucifix and Virgin was a small
Photo of *la Mamma*——which surveyed,
With madamely aplomb, the girls he'd laid.
(Note also: right below the feet of God,
A shelf with hair oil and *Justine* by Sade.)

The Perfect Poet

He says he is a perfect poet.
He lives alone, with his perfect mate.
& sometimes they don't even speak,
So perfectly do they "communicate."

He lives alone, his greatest pleasures are
His pipes, his books, his wife's behind—
Which he will often pinch to hear her laugh;
He's got a perfect love for womankind.

He seldom writes, distrusting language as
A clumsy tool, unequal to his thoughts:
He uses it as rarely as he can
(No doubt to punish it for all its faults).

But when he writes, he keeps the upper hand
(On principle, since words are enemies).
He melts them down, then counterfeits his own—
A kind of literary alchemy.

He's fortunate to have a perfect muse.
A live-in muse, who cooks inspiringly;
And sometimes after an ambrosial meal,
He'll grab his pen, composing feverishly

A perfect poem, describing in detail
The salad, wine, the roast in buttery baste.
And reading it, his musing wife agrees
That every line smacks of his perfect taste.

Autumn Perspective

Now, moving in, cartons on the floor,
the radio playing to bare walls,
picture hooks left stranded
in the unsoiled squares where paintings were,
and something reminding us
this is like all other moving days;
finding the dirty ends of someone else's life,
hair fallen in the sink, a peach pit,
and burned-out matches in a corner;
things not preserved, yet never swept away
like fragments of disturbing dreams
we stumble on all day . . .
in ordering our lives, we will discard them,
scrub clean the floorboards of this our home
lest refuse from the lives we did not lead
become, in some strange, frightening way, our own.
And we have plans that will not tolerate
our fears—a year laid out like rooms
in a new house—the dusty wine glasses
rinsed off, the vases filled, and bookshelves
sagging with the heavy winter books.
Seeing the room always as it will be,
we are content to dust and wait.
We will return here from the dark and silent
streets, arms full of books and food,
anxious as we always are in winter,
and looking for the Good Life we have made.

I see myself then: tense, solemn,
in high-heeled shoes that pinch,
not basking in the light of goals fulfilled,
but looking back to now and seeing
a lazy, sunburned, sandaled girl
in a bare room, full of promise
and feeling envious.

Now we plan, postponing, pushing our lives forward
into the future—as if, when the room
contains us and all our treasured junk
we will have filled whatever gap it is
that makes us wander, discontented
from ourselves.

The room will not change:
a rug, or armchair, or new coat of paint
won't make much difference;
our eyes are fickle
but we remain the same beneath our suntans,
pale, frightened,
dreaming ourselves backward and forward in time,
dreaming our dreaming selves.

I look forward and see myself look back.

The Nazi Amphitheatre

Abandoned by their parents
in a wood,
Hansel & Gretel
found this place:
a child's nightmare
run wild with weeds;
blank stage for the hero,
seats stepping off:
optical illusions;
poles for flags flapping:
cheering tongues;
pines bayonetting the sky;
a forest formed
of all the fears
in night's imagination.

Now we come upon it hand in hand,
see nothing but an earthen bowl
littered with bottle bits
& condom wrappers,
disowned by the town,
harangued by rain,
the focus of conflicting
memories. ("Hitler spoke here."
"No, he never did.")
——As if it mattered.

This place is a house
bought by a manic
& not remembered
later in the asylum.
Invisible from the city,
forgotten in a gothic forest,
it waits for Hansel & Gretel
(us perhaps) to wake up,
dreaming some recurrent dream.

By Train from Berlin

A delicate border. A nonexistent country.
The train obligingly dissolves in smoke.
The G.I. next to me is talking war.
I don't "know the Asian mind," he says.

Moving through old arguments.

At Potsdam (a globe-shaped dome,
a pink canal reflecting sepia trees)
we pull next to a broken-down old train
with REICHSBAHN lettered on its flank.

Thirty years sheer away leaving bare cliff.

This is a country I don't recognize.
Bone-pale girls who have nothing to do with home.
Everyone's taller than me, everyone naked.
"Life's cheap there," he says.

But why are we screaming over a track
which runs between a barbed wire corridor?
And why has it grown so dark outside,
so bright in here

that even the pared moon is invisible?

In the window we can only see ourselves,
America we carry with us,
two scared people talking death
on a train which can't stop.

Near the Black Forest

Living in a house
near the Black Forest,
without any clocks,
she's begun

to listen to the walls.
Her neighbors have clocks,
not one
but twenty clocks apiece.

Sometimes
a claque of clocks
applauds
the passing of each day.

Listen to the walls
& wind your watch.
Poor love, poor love,
have they caught you

by the pendulum?
Do they think they've
got you stopped?
Have you

already gathered how,
living near the Black Forest,
she gets by
on cups of borrowed time?

The Artist as an Old Man

If you ask him he will talk for hours—
how at fourteen he hammered signs, fingers
raw with cold, and later painted bowers
in ladies' boudoirs; how he played checkers
for two weeks in jail, and lived on dark bread;
how he fled the border to a country
which disappeared wars ago; unfriended
crossed a continent while this century
began. He seldom speaks of painting now.
Young men have time and theories; old men work.
He has painted countless portraits. Sallow
nameless faces, made glistening in oil, smirk
above anonymous mantelpieces.
The turpentine has a familiar smell,
but his hand trembles with odd, new palsies.
Perched on the maulstick, it nears the easel.

He has come to like his resignation.
In his sketch books, ink-dark cossacks hear
the snorts of horses in the crunch of snow.
His pen alone recalls that years ago,
one horseman set his teeth and aimed his spear
which, poised, seemed pointed straight to pierce the sun.

The Catch

You take me to the restaurant where one
plays god over a fish tank. The fat trout
pace their green cage, waiting to be taken
out of an element. Who knows what they know?
There are thirteen in a tank meant
for goldfish. I don't care which one I eat.

But the waiter expects a performance,
con brio. This is a ritual
solemn as wine-tasting or the Last Judgment.
Eating is never so simple as hunger.
Between the appetite and its satisfaction
falls the net, groping blindly in dark water.

The fish startle and thrash. You make your catch,
flourishing a bit for the waiter
so as not to be thought a peasant. You force
air into the trout's gills as if he were Adam,
and send him squirming toward the kitchen
to be born. Then it's my turn. I surprise

myself with my dexterity, almost
enjoying the game. A liter of wine
later, the fish return, foppishly dressed
in mushrooms and pimentos, their eyes
dreamily hazed. Darling, I am drunk. I watch you pluck

the trout's ribs out of your perfect teeth.

At the Museum of Natural History

The lessons we learned here
(fumbling with our lunchbags,
handkerchiefs
& secret cheeks of bubblegum)

were graver than any
in the schoolroom:
the dangers of a life
frozen into poses.

Trilobites in their
petrified ghettos,
lumbering dinosaurs
who'd outsized themselves

told how nature was
an endless morality play
in which the cockroach
(& all such beadyeyed

exemplars of adjustment)
might well recite the epilogue.
No one was safe
but stagnation was

the surest suicide.
To mankind's Hamlet,
what six-legged creature would play
Fortinbras? It made you scratch

your head & think
for about two minutes.
Going out, I remember
how we stopped to look at

Teddy Roosevelt,
(Soldier, Statesman, Naturalist,
Hunter, Historian,
et cetera, et cetera).

His bronze bulk (four times life size)
bestrode Central Park West
like a colossus.
His monumental horse

snorted towards the park.
Oh, we were full of Evolution & its lessons
when (the girls giggling madly,

the boys blushing) we peeked
between those huge legs to see
those awe-inspiring
Brobdingnagian balls.

To James Boswell in London

Boswell—you old rake—I have tried to imitate
your style; but it is no use; my dialogues are
all between my selves: and though I sit up late,
make endless notes and jottings that I hope will jar
my memory—it is in vain—for in the end
I have no Dr. Johnson but myself.

The difference is (I think) between our lives. You spend
the morning at the coffee house, nourish yourself
with talk and kippers before proceeding on to dine.
A ramble across London perks the appetite.
Every step is an adventure; the written line
distills itself from life. How can you help but write?

I consort with books while you see men, haunt the shelves
where your London lies buried. Your book once opened,
I become the ghost, a pale phantom who delves
into your life to borrow moments penned
two hundred years ago. I roam your world ignored—
while my own life, waiting outside, questions my motives.

A man should never live more than he can record
you say; but what if he records more than he *lives?*
My journal swarms with me and even I am bored.
I am all my personae—children, lovers, wives,
philosophers and country-wenches. Though I give them
different robes and wigs to wear, all converse alike;

all reason falsely with the same stratagem;
each suspects the logic of the other, dislikes
him, yet cannot prove him wrong. Petty cavils
grow to monstrous issues, belabored arguments
resolve themselves only in sleep; darkness prevails.
Only the living find solace in common sense.

Safe, preserved from the rape of the world, I grow
dishonest, and pen my crooked words, for one can lie
with ease about those things the world will never know.
Conversation—that clearinghouse for thoughts—denied,
the mind gets gouty and the conscience needs a cane.
Notions unuttered seem to echo through the brain—
and our monologues are doomed to the same end.
We all think better—interrupted by a friend.

Death of a Romantic

He died in Rome, in all that sunlight,
the Spanish Steps full of trysting lovers,
Bernini's watery boat still sinking
in the fountain in the square below.
And even if they weren't lovers
who crowded the burning steps that day—
but businessmen complaining of the heat,
tired tourists or prowling gigolos—
he had to bear his dark delirium
while the world breathed and sweated outside.

It was no day to die—his tongue dumb
with fever, and all his senses raging
out of tune—The slow *continuo*
of fountains, weakly pulsing,
a disembodied rhythm robbed of song—
and all that unexpected, wide-flung sky
shattered hourly by bells, the frenzied
flapping of a lone bird's wings
—determined—in a wilderness of air.

The sunlight fades now, eyes bound burning
within their fleshy lids—they close to see
kaleidoscopes of light, the spectrum suns,
—those fiery self-consuming hearts that blaze
one final time, against finality
like embers flaring in a gust of breath
—when death—the silent, steadfast muse,
the faithful lover—comes to consummate
a long flirtation.

Eveningsong at Bellosguardo

Chi vuol esser lieto, sia:
di doman non c'e certezza.

—Lorenzo di Medici

In the poplars' lengthening shadows on this hill,
amid the rows of marigolds and earth,
and through the boxhedge labyrinth we walk,
together, to the choiring twilight bells.
Their fugue of echoes echoes through the hills
and sings against this time-streaked, flowering wall
where breezes coax the potted lemon trees,
the pendant, yellow fruit and shiny leaves.
Beneath the flaming watercolor sky,
the cultivated, terraced drop of hill,
a gleaming city with its towers and domes,
the Arno shimmering as it drowns the sun.

Chameleon-like, I am transformed by light,
and wine has blurred the edges of the night.
What gifts I give on this or any night
may be refracted in another light.
You understand this in a foreign tongue,
but vaguely, for these things will not translate.
I feel it in the cadence of your walk:
you are not one whom moonlight can create.
And you will think the loosening of these thighs,
the sudden, urging whiteness of the throat

are muted but distinctly pagan cries
and in your triumph you will fairly gloat.

Tonight the unplucked lemons almost gleam.
And with their legs, the crickets harmonize.
The trees are rustling an uncertain hymn,
and unseen birds contribute trembling cries.
When did the summer censor choiring things?
We know the blood is brutal though it sings.

On Sending You a Lock of My Hair

There is a white wood house near Hampstead Heath
in whose garden the nightingale still sings.
Though Keats is dead, the bird who sang of death
returns with melodies, on easeful wings.

A lock of hair the poet's love received
remains in the room where first it was shorn;
An heirloom, its history half-believed,
its strands now faded and its ribbon worn.

On polished floors, through squares of summer sun
I felt his footsteps move, as if the elf
—deceiving elf, he called her—had not done
with making mischief to amuse herself.

I saw him clip that tousled lock of hair,
and though he did not offer it to me,
I felt that I was privileged, standing there,
and took his gesture for my legacy.

In Defense of the English Portrait School

Apologists blame it on the English
temperament, which "unable to conceive
the monumental," called for stylish
portraits of the rich. The critics forgive
Gainsborough, considering the bad taste
of his patrons: if you squint and pretend
that the satin isn't satin, a feast
of color awaits you, they recommend.
The stoop-shouldered young men with knotted brows
walk through the English gallery sullenly,
still denying the sun-dappled meadows
of a vanished upper class. A lady
Lawrence painted dangles gloves of amber
suede between fingers slim from idleness;
Her satin cape blowing in October
wind is heavy, silvery white and soundless,
addressing itself to clouds of similar
stuff. She looks away unmindful that she
is not profound, or even popular.
Across from her a rake whose pedigree
is told in the knowing curl of his lip,
slaps the sleek rump of his burnished brown mare.
He holds a leather crop and at his hip
his watch fob glints; he waits and on a dare
he'd take the pasture at a gallop, jump
the highest fences, hooves making hollows
in the echoing air. Three children, plump
with laughter, are busy feeding sparrows

on another canvas. They toss their heads
to shake their curls with sunlight, stretch their arms
to show their puckered hands. The boy who spreads
the bread crumbs on the ground, quietly disarms
us, though we know he probably grew old,
deserved his gout, had a borough in each
pocket, and unknowing died a cuckold.
It is his splendid childhood we reproach
by thinking of the vices he was heir to;
envy calling history as witness
to taint the boyish smile the artist drew.

Oh leave the poor aristocrats in peace!
No one is fooled, for Hogarth painted too;
and though not democratic, art can please—
the cavil is absurd, the colors true.

To X. (With Ephemeral Kisses)

I hear you will not fall in love with me
because I come without a guarantee,
because someday I may depart at whim
and leave you desolate, abandoned, grim.
If that's the case, what use to be alive?
In loving life you love what can't survive:
and if you grow too fond and lose your head,
it's all for nought—for someday you'll be dead.
Maintain a cool detachment through the years.
Wear blinders, dear, put cotton in your ears.
Since worms will taste the tongue that tastes the wine,
burst not the grape against your palate fine.
With care, your puny heart will still be whole
the day they come to fetch your tepid soul.
And as that strumpet, Life, deals her last blow,
you'll have this final *consolatio:*
you'll snap your flippant fingers as you fall,
and say, "I never cared for *her* at all!"

The Lives of the Poets: Three Profiles

I.

He was content to speak of little things—
the sound of raindrops on a roof, the scent
of spring, a field of haystacks, a hill
of cherry trees, a pebble's smoothness
or a thrush's wings; nor ever seemed to care
that nations fought, that men and women loved,
that young men died, that scholars quarreled,
that politicians lied, that children hungered
while their mothers cried. But what he spoke of
(it cannot be denied) he spoke of sweetly
and he never falsified. With all good cheer
he took his limitation, and never risked
his pen on any side. His silence was
the bulk of his creation: he held his tongue
too much, perhaps, but then, he never lied.

II.

By birth, upbringing, inclination,
he made his task the mastery of words,
became the spokesman for his generation,
and reaped from that the double-edged rewards.
Through two world wars he railed against the lie
that bloodshed ever serves a noble cause,
saw anarchy invade, and made reply,
by praising order, harmony and law.
Likewise when famine struck, when children died,

when innocents were sentenced without trial,
he always let his conscience be his guide—
though critics claimed it much impaired his style.
Throughout a long career of writing verse,
he often changed his mind; men have the right;
exchanged his benedictions for a curse,
transformed his politics from left to right.
Although his prophet's cape did not quite fit,
although he made mistakes because he dared,
he chronicled his age with biting wit,
and though he did not change the world, he cared.

III.

He had no complex notion of aesthetics.
He liked his food well-spiced, his women fair;
he had a kind of passion for athletics,
and at the age of sixty, all his hair.
He worshipped music and he liked to drink,
was fond of travel, company, long walks;
he could not bear to be alone to think,
and best of all, he dearly loved to talk.
It's doubtful how he chose his occupation;
he thought that routine work was Adam's curse.
He had some money, and a talent for narration
and one day tried his hand at writing verse.
His ear for words was almost never wrong;
he liked applause and reveled in his fame.
Whatever crossed his mind became a song,
and yet he half-conceived his craft a game.
In all his poems there seemed to be the hint
that had his stay on earth been better timed,
he would have rushed to battle, not to print,
but since there was no Troy to fight, he rhymed.

III

❖

Fruits & Vegetables

(1971)

Fruits & Vegetables

1

Goodbye, he waved, entering the apple.
That red siren,
whose white flesh turns brown
with prolonged exposure to air,
opened her perfect cheeks to receive him.
She took him in.
The garden revolved
in her glossy patinas of skin.
Goodbye.

2

O note the two round holes in onion.

3

Did I tell you about
my mother's avocado?
She grew it from a pit.
Secretly, slowly in the dark,
it put out grub-white roots
which filled a jelly jar.
From this unlikely start,
an avocado tree with bark
& dark green leaves
shaded the green silk couch
which shaded me

throughout my shady adolescence.
There, beneath that tree
my skirt gave birth to hands!
Oh memorable hands of boys
with blacked-out eyes
like culprits
in the *National Enquirer.*
My mother nursed that tree
like all her children,
turned it around so often
towards the sun
that its trunk grew twisted
as an old riverbed,
& despite its gaudy leaves
it never bore
fruit.

4

Cantaloupes: the setting sun at Paestum
slashed by rosy columns.

5

I am thinking of the onion again, with its two O mouths, like the gaping
holes in nobody. Of the outer skin, pinkish brown, peeled to reveal a
greenish sphere, bald as a dead planet, glib as glass, & an odor almost
animal. I consider its ability to draw tears, its capacity for self-scrutiny,
flaying itself away, layer on layer, in search of its heart which is simply
another region of skin, but deeper & greener. I remember Peer Gynt. I
consider its sometimes double heart. Then I think of despair when the
onion searches its soul & finds only its various skins; & I think of the dried
tuft of roots leading nowhere & the parched umbilicus, lopped off in the
garden. Not self-righteous like the proletarian potato, nor a siren like the
apple. No show-off like the banana. But a modest, self-effacing vegetable,
questioning, introspective, peeling itself away, or merely radiating halos
like lake ripples. I consider it the eternal outsider, the middle child, the
sad analysand of the vegetable kingdom. Glorified only in France (other-
wise silent sustainer of soups & stews), unloved for itself alone——no

wonder it draws our tears! Then I think again how the outer peel
resembles paper, how soul & skin merge into one, how each peeling
strips bare a heart which in turn turns skin . . .

6

A poet in a world without onions,
in a world without apples
regards the earth as a great fruit.

Far off, galaxies glitter like currants.
The whole edible universe drops
to his watering mouth . . .

Think of generations of mystics
salivating for the fruit of god,
of poets yearning to inhabit apples,
of the sea, that dark fruit,
closing much more quickly than a wound,
of the nameless galaxies of astronomers,
hoping that the cosmos will ripen
& their eyes will become tongues . . .

7

For the taste of the fruit
is the tongue's dream,
& the apple's red
is the passion of the eye.

8

If a woman wants to be a poet,
she must dwell in the house of the tomato.

9

It is not an emptiness,
the fruit between your legs,
but the long hall of history,

& dreams are coming down the hall
by moonlight.

10

They push up through the loam
like lips of mushrooms.

11

(Artichoke, after Child): Holding the heart base up, rotate it slowly with your left hand against the blade of a knife held firmly in your right hand to remove all pieces of ambition & expose the pale surface of the heart. Frequently rub the cut portions with gall. Drop each heart as it is finished into acidulated water. The choke can be removed after cooking.

12

(Artichoke, after Neruda)

It is green at the artichoke heart,
but remember the times
you flayed
leaf after leaf,
hoarding the pale silver paste
behind the fortresses of your teeth,
tonguing the vinaigrette,
only to find the husk of a worm
at the artichoke heart?
The palate reels like a wronged lover.
Was all that sweetness counterfeit?
Must you vomit back
world after vegetable world
for the sake of one worm
in the green garden of the heart?

13

But the poem about bananas has not yet been written. Southerners worry a lot about bananas. Their skin. And nearly everyone worries about the size of bananas, as if that had anything to do with flavor. Small bananas are sometimes quite sweet. But bananas are like poets: they only want to be told how great they are. Green bananas want to be told they're ripe. According to Freud, girls envy bananas. In America, chocolate syrup & whipped cream have been known to enhance the flavor of bananas. This is called a *banana split*.

14

The rice is pregnant.
It swells past its old transparency.
Hard, translucent worlds inside the grains
open like fans. It is raining rice!
The peasants stand under oiled
rice paper umbrellas cheering.

Someone is scattering rice from the sky!
Chopper blades mash the clouds.
The sky browns like cheese soufflé.
Rice grains puff & pop open.

"What have we done to deserve this?"
the peasants cry. Even the babies
are cheering. Cheers slide from their lips
like spittle. Old men kick their clogs
into the air & run in the rice paddies
barefoot. This is a monsoon! A wedding!

Each grain has a tiny invisible parachute.
Each grain is a rain drop.

"They have sent us rice!" the mothers scream,
opening their throats to the smoke . . .

15

Here should be a picture of my favorite apple.
It is also a nude & bottle.

It is also a landscape.
There are no such things as still lives.

16

In general, modern poetry requires (underline one): a) more fruit; b) less
fruit; c) more vegetables; d) less vegetables; e) all of the above; f) none
of the above.

17

Astonishment of apples. Every fall.
But only Italians are into grapes,
calling them *eggs*.
O my eggs,
branching off my family tree,
my father used to pluck you,
leaving bare twigs on the dining room table,
leaving mother furious on the dining room table:
picked clean.
Bare ruined choirs
where late the sweet.
A pile of pits.

18

Adam naming the fruit
after the creation of fruit,
his tongue tickling
the crimson lips of the pomegranate,
the tip of his penis licking
the cheeks of the peach,
quince petals in his hair,
his blue arms full of plums,
his legs wrapped around watermelons,
dandling pumpkins on his fatherly knees,
tomatoes heaped around him in red pyramids . .

peach
peach
peach
peach
peach

he sighs

to kingdom come.

The Man Under the Bed

The man under the bed
The man who has been there for years waiting
The man who waits for my floating bare foot
The man who is silent as dustballs riding the darkness
The man whose breath is the breathing of small white butterflies
The man whose breathing I hear when I pick up the phone
The man in the mirror whose breath blackens silver
The boneman in closets who rattles the mothballs
The man at the end of the end of the line

I met him tonight   I always meet him
He stands in the amber air of a bar
When the shrimp curl like beckoning fingers
& ride through the air on their toothpick skewers
When the ice cracks & I am about to fall through
he arranges his face around its hollows
he opens his pupilless eyes at me
For years he has waited to drag me down
& now he tells me
he has only waited to take me home
We waltz through the street like death & the maiden
We float through the wall of the wall of my room

If he's my dream he will fold back into my body
His breath writes letters of mist on the glass of my cheeks
I wrap myself around him like the darkness
I breathe into his mouth
& make him real

Walking Through the Upper East Side

All over the district, on leather couches
& brocade couches, on daybeds
& "professional divans," they are confessing.
The air is thick with it,
the ears of the analysts must be sticky.

Words fill the air above couches & hover there
hanging like smog. I imagine
impossible Steinberg scrolls,
unutterable sounds suspended in inked curlicues
while the Braque print & the innocuous Utrillo
look on look on look on.

My six analysts, for example—

the sly Czech who tucked his shoelaces
under the tongues of his shoes,
the mistress of social work with orange hair,
the famous old German who said:
"You sink, zerefore you are,"
the bouncy American who loved to talk dirty,
the bitchy widow of a famous theoretician,
& another—or was it two?—I have forgotten—
they rise like a Greek chorus in my dreams.
They reproach me for my messy life.
They do not offer to refund my money.

& the others——siblings for an hour or so——
ghosts whom I brushed in & out of the door.
Sometimes the couch was warm from their bodies.
Only our coats knew each other,
rubbing shoulders in the dark closet.

Here Comes

The silver spoons
were warbling
their absurd musical names
when, drawing back
her veil (illusion),

she stepped into
the valentine-shaped bathtub,
& slid her perfect bubbles
in between
the perfect bubbles.

Oh brilliantly complex as
compound interest,
her diamond gleams
(Forever) on the edge
of a weddingcake-shaped bed.

What happens there
is merely icing since
a snakepit of dismembered
douchebag coils (all writhing)
awaits her on the tackier back pages.

Dearly beloved, let's hymn
her (& Daddy) down
the aisle with
epithalamia composed
for Ovulen ads:

"It's the right
of every (married) couple
to wait   to space   to wait"
—& antistrophes
appended by the Pope.

Good Grief—the groom!
Has she (or we)
entirely forgot?
She'll dream him whole.
American type with ushers

halfbacks headaches drawbacks backaches
& borrowed suit
stuffed in a borrowed face
(or was it the reverse?)
Oh well. Here's he:

part coy pajamas,
part mothered underwear
& of course
an enormous prick
full of money.

The Commandments

You don't really want to be a poet. First of
all, if you're a woman, you have to be
three *times as good as any of the men.*
Secondly, you have to fuck everyone. And
thirdly, you have to be dead.

—Mark Strand, in conversation

If a woman wants to be a poet,
   she should sleep near the moon with her face open;
   she should walk through herself studying the landscape;
   she should not write her poems in menstrual blood.

If a woman wants to be a poet,
   she should run backwards circling the volcano;
   she should feel for the movement along her faults;
   she should not get a Ph.D. in seismography.

If a woman wants to be a poet,
   she should not sleep with uncircumcised manuscripts;
   she should not write odes to her abortions;
   she should not make stew of old unicorn meat.

If a woman wants to be a poet,
   she should read French cookbooks and Chinese vegetables;
   she should suck on French poets to freshen her breath;
   she should not masturbate in writing seminars.

If a woman wants to be a poet,
    she should peel back the hair from her eyeballs;
    she should listen to the breathing of sleeping men;
    she should listen to the spaces between that breathing.

If a woman wants to be a poet,
    she should not write her poems with a dildo;
    she should pray that her daughters are women;
    she should forgive her father for his bravest sperm.

Aging

(balm for a 27th birthday)

Hooked for two years now on wrinkle creams   creams for
crowsfeet   ugly lines (if only there were one!)
any perfumed grease   which promises   youth   beauty
not truth   but all I need on earth
         I've been studying   how women age

            how

it starts around the eyes   so you can tell
a woman of 22 from one of 28 merely by
a faint scribbling near the lids   a subtle crinkle
      a fine line
extending from the fields of vision

            this

in itself is not unbeautiful   promising
      as it often does
insights which clear-eyed 22 has no inkling of
promising   certain sure-thighed things in bed
certain fingers on your spine & lids

            but

it's only the beginning   as ruin proceeds downward
lingering for a while around the mouth   hardening the smile
into prearranged patterns (irreversible!)   writing furrows
from the wings of the nose   (oh nothing much at first
          but "showing promise"   like your early poems

                    of deepening)

& plotting lower to the corners of the mouth   drooping them
a little   like the tragic mask   though not at all grotesque
as yet   & then as you sidestep   into the 4th decade
beginning to crease the neck   (just slightly)
          though the breasts below

                    especially

When they're small (like mine) may stay high far
          into the thirties
still the neck will give you away   & after that the chin
which   though you may snip it back & hike it up under
your earlobes will never quite love your bones as it once did

                    though

the belly may be kept firm through numerous pregnancies
by means of sit-ups   jogging   dancing   (think of Russian
ballerinas)
          & the cunt
as far as I know is ageless   possibly immortal
becoming simply
more open   more quick to understand   more dry-eyed
than at 22

                    which

after all   is what you were dying for   (as you ravaged
islands of turtles   beehives   oysterbeds   the udders of
cows)

desperate to censor changes which you simply might have let play
over you   lying back   listening   opening yourself
        letting the years make love the only way   (poor
    blunderers)

                        they know

In Sylvia Plath Country

for Grace

The skin of the sea
has nothing to tell me.

I see her diving down
into herself—

past the bell-shaped jellyfish
who toll for no one—

& meaning to come back.

❖

In London, in the damp
of a London morning,
I see her sitting,
folding & unfolding herself,
while the blood
hammers like rain
on her heart's windows.

This is her own country—
the sea, the rain
& death half rhyming
with her father's name.

Obscene monosyllable,
it lingers for a while
on the roof
of the mouth's house.

I stand here
savoring the sound,
like salt.

❖

They thought your death
was your last poem:
a black book
with gold-tooled cover
& pages the color of ash.

But I thought different,
knowing how madness
doesn't believe
in metaphor.

When you began to feel
the drift of continents
beneath your feet,
the sea's suck,
& each
atom of the poisoned air,
you lost
the luxury of simile.

Gull calls, broken shells,
the quarried coast.
This is where America ends,
dropping off
to the depths.

Death comes
differently in California.

Marilyn stalled
in celluloid,
the frame stuck,
& the light
burning through.

Bronze to her platinum,
Ondine, Ariel,
finally no one,

what could we tell you
after you dove down into yourself
& were swallowed
by your poems?

A Reading

The old poet
with his face full of lines,
with iambs jumping in his hair like fleas,
with all the revisions of his body
unsaying him,
walks to the podium.

He is about to tell us
how he came to this.

Imaginary Landscapes

for my parents

Who are these small determined figures
            with turbaned heads
                        coming
to doric temples
            in
                        fifteenth-century galleons
            with
medieval castles
                        in the background?
      They speak
                        & gesture in the halflight,
                                    bring
                  cattle, parcels
                              to the classic shore
            below the gothic hill.
                        Sunlight moonlight twilight starlight
gleams across
                  a stagey sea.
                              Clouds toss. Sails fill.
      Windlessly,
                        what banners wave?
                  Whose landscape
                              is this mind?

Whose bluish breasts became
           these castled hills?
                    Whose darkness is
     this winter afternoon?
Whose darkness is
          this darkening gallery?
    Turn softly mind, wind,
               Claude Lorrain,
   Turner's making
        light of Venice,
   showing
     his true
       colors.

The Saturday Market

For Alexander Mitscherlich

Lumbering down
in the early morning clatter
from farms
where the earth was hard all winter,
the market women bear
grapes blue as the veins
of fair-skinned women,
cherries dark as blood,
roses strewn like carnage
on makeshift altars.
They come
in ancient rattling trucks
which sprout geraniums,
are stained
with strawberries.
Their fingers thick
& thorn-pricked,
their huge smock-pockets
jingling pennies,
they walk,
heavy goddesses,
while the market
blossoms into bleeding
all round them.
Currants which glitter

like Christmas ornaments
are staining
their wooden boxes.
Cherries, grapes—
everything
seems to be bleeding!
I think
how a sentimental
German poet
might have written
that the cut rose
mourns the garden
& the grapes
their Rhineland vineyard
(where the crooked vines
stretch out their arms
like dancers)
for this
is a sentimental country
& Germans
are passionate gardeners
who view with humanity
the blights of roses,
the adversities of vineyards.
But I am not fooled.
This bleeding is, no doubt,
in the beholder's eye,
& if
to tend a garden
is to be civilized,
surely this country
of fat cabbages
& love-lavished geraniums
would please
an eighteenth-century
philosopher.
Two centuries, however,
buzz above my head

like hornets over fruit.
I stuff my mouth with cherries
as I watch
the thorn-pricked fingers
of the market women
lifting & weighing,
weighing, weighing.

The Heidelberg Landlady

Because she lost her father
in the First World War,
her husband in the Second,
we don't dispute
"There's no *Gemütlichkeit* in America."

We're winning her heart
with filter cigarettes.
Puffing, she says,
"You can't judge a country
by just twelve years."

Gray days,
the wind hobbling down sidestreets,
I'm walking in a thirties photograph,
the prehistoric age
before my birth.

This town was never bombed.
Old ladies still wear funny shoes,
long, seedy furs.
They smell of camphor and camomile,
old photographs.

Nothing much happened here.
A few jewelry shops changed hands.
A brewery. Banks.
The university put up a swastika, took it down.

125

The students now chant HO CHI MINH & hate Americans
on principle.
Daddy wears a flyer's cap
& never grew old.
He's on the table with the teacakes.
Mother & grandma are widows.

They take care of things.
It rains nearly every day;
every day, they wash the windows.
They cultivate jungles in the front parlors,
lush tropics

framed by lacy white curtains.
They coax the earth with plant food, scrub the leaves.
Each plant shines like a fat child.
They hope for the sun,
living in a Jewless world without men.

Student Revolution

(Heidelberg, 1969)

After the teach-in
we smeared the walls with
our solidarity,
looked left, & saw
Marx among the angels,
singing the blues.

The students march,
I (spectator)
follow.
Here (as everywhere)
the *Polizei*
are clean, are clean.

In Frankfurt,
the whores lean out
their windows, screaming:
"Get a job—you dirty
hippies!" Or words
(auf Deutsch) to that effect.

I'm also waiting
for the Revolution,
friends.
Surely, my poems

will get better.
Surely, I'll no longer
fear my dreams.
Surely I won't murder
my capitalist father
each night
just to inherit
his love.

Flying You Home

*I only remember the onion, the egg and the
boy. O that was me, said the madman.*

—Nicholas Moore

1

"I bite into an apple & then get bored
before the second bite," you said.
You were also Samson. I had cut
your hair & locked you up.
Besides, your room was bugged.
A former inmate left his muse
spread-eagled on the picture window.
In the glinting late-day sun
we saw her huge & cross-eyed breasts appear
diamond-etched
against the slums of Harlem.
You tongued your pills & cursed the residents.
You called me Judas.
You forgot I was a girl.

2

Your hands weren't birds. To call
them birds would be too easy.
They drew circles around your ideas
& your ideas were sometimes parabolas.
That sudden Sunday you awoke
& found yourself behind the looking glass,

your hands perched on the breakfast table
waiting for a sign.
I had nothing to tell them.
They conversed with the eggs.

3

We walked.
Your automatic umbrella snapped
into place above your head
like a black halo.
We thought of climbing down rain puddles
as if they were manholes.
You said the reflected buildings
led to hell.
Trees danced for us,
cut-out people turned sideways
& disappeared into their voices.
The cities in our glasses took us in.
You stood on a scale, heard the penny drop—
but the needle was standing still!
It proved that you were God.

4

The elevator opens & reveals me
holding African violets.
An hour later I vanish
into a chasm whose dimensions
are 23 hours.
Tranquilized, brittle,
you strut the corridors
among the dapper young psychiatrists,
the girls who weave rugs all day,
unravel them all night,
the obesity cases lost in themselves.
You hum. You say you hate me.
I would like to shake you.
Remember how it happened?

You were standing at the window
speaking about flying.
Your hands flew to my throat.
When they came they found
our arms strewn around the floor
like broken toys.
We both were crying.

5

You stick. Somewhere in a cellar of my mind,
you stick. Fruit spoke to you
before it spoke to me. Apples cried
when you peeled them.
Tangerines jabbered in Japanese.
You stared into an oyster
& sucked out God.
You were the hollow man,
with Milton entering your left foot.

6

My first husband!——God——
you've become an abstraction,
a kind of idea. I can't even hear
your voice anymore. Only the black hair
curled on your belly makes you real—
I draw black curls on all the men I write.
I don't even look anymore.

7

I thought of you in Istanbul.
Your Byzantine face,
thin lips & hollow cheeks,
the fanatical melting brown eyes.
In Hagia Sophia they're stripping down
the moslem plaster
to find mosaics underneath.

The pieces fit in place.
You'd have been a Saint.

8

I'm good at interiors.
Gossip, sharpening edges, kitchen poems—
& have no luck at all with maps.
It's because of being a woman
& having everything inside.
I decorated the cave,
hung it with animal skins & woolens,
such soft floors,
that when you fell
you thought you fell on me.
You had a perfect sense of bearings
to the end,
were always pointing North.

9

Flying you home—
good Christ—flying you home,
you were terrified.
You held my hand, I held
my father's hand & he
filched pills from the psychiatrist
who'd come along for you.
The psychiatrist was 26 & scared.
He hoped I'd keep you calm.
& so we flew.
Hand in hand in hand in hand we flew.

Books

The universe (which others call the library) . . .

—Jorge Luis Borges

Books which are stitched up the center with coarse white thread
Books on the beach with sunglass-colored pages
Books about food with pictures of weeping grapefruits
Books about baking bread with browned corners
Books about long-haired Frenchmen with uncut pages
Books of erotic engravings with pages that stick
Books about inns whose stars have sputtered out
Books of illuminations surrounded by darkness
Books with blank pages & printed margins
Books with fanatical footnotes in no-point type
Books with book lice
Books with rice-paper pastings
Books with book fungus blooming over their pages
Books with pages of skin with flesh-colored bindings
Books by men in love with the letter O
Books which smell of earth whose pages turn

IV

❖

FROM

Half-Lives

(1973)

The Evidence

1

Evidence of life:
snapshots,
hundreds of split-seconds
when the eyes glazed over,
the hair stopped its growing,
the nails froze in fingertips,
the blood hung suspended
in its vessels—

while the small bloodships,
the red & white bloodboats
buoyed up & down at anchor
like the toys
of millionaires. . . .

Evidence of life:
a split-second's death
to live forever
in something called
a *print.*
A paparazzo life:
I shoot therefore I am.

2

Why does life need evidence
of life?

We disbelieve it
even as we live.

The bloodboats gently rocking,
the skull opening every night
to dreams more vivid than itself,
more solid
than its own bones,
the brain flowering with petals,
stamens, pistils,
magical fruit
which reproduces
from its own juice,
which invents
its own mouth,
& makes itself anew
each night.

3

Evidence of life?
My dreams.
The dreams which I write down.
The dreams which I relate
each morning with a solemn face
inventing as I go.

Evidence of life:
that we could meet for the first time,
open our scars & stitches to each other,
weave our legs around
each other's patchwork dreams
& try to salve each other's wounds
with love—

if it was love.

(I am not sure at all
if love is salve
or just
a deeper kind of wound.
I do not think it matters.)

If it was lust or hunger
& not love,
if it was all that they accused us of
(that we accused ourselves)—
I do not think it matters.

4

Evidence of love?
I imagine our two heads
sliced open like grapefruits,
pressed each half to half
& mingling acid juice
in search of sweet.

I imagine all my dreams
sliding out into your open skull—
as if I were the poet,
you the reader.

I imagine all your dreams
pressed against my belly
like your sperm
& singing into me.

I imagine my two hands
cupped around your life
& stroking it.

I imagine your two hands
making whirlpools

in my blood,
then quelling them.

5

I have no photograph of you.
At times I hardly can believe in you.
Except this ache,
this longing in my gut,
this emptiness which theorizes you
because if there is emptiness this deep,
there must be fullness somewhere.

My other half!
My life beyond this half-life!

Is life a wound
which dreams of being healed?

Is love a wound which deepens
as it dreams?

Do you exist?
Evidence:
these poems in which
I have been conjuring you,
this book which makes your absence palpable,
these longings printed black.
I am exposed.
I am a print of darkness
on a square of film.
I am a garbled dream
told by a breakfast-table liar.
I am a wound which has forgotten how to heal.

6

& if it wasn't love,
if you called me now

across the old echo chamber of the ocean
& said:
"Look, I never loved you,"
I would feel
a little like a fool perhaps,
& yet it wouldn't matter.

My business is to always feel
a little like a fool
& speak of it.

& I am sure
that when we love
we are better than ourselves
& when we hate,
worse.

& even if we call it madness later
& scrawl four-letter words
across those outhouse walls
we call our skulls—
we stand revealed
by those sudden moments
when we come together.

7

Evidence?
Or was it just my dream
waltzing with your dream?
My nightmare kissing yours?

When I awakened
did I walk with Jacob's limp?
Did I sing a different song?
Did I find the inside of my palm
scarred as if
(for moments) it held fire?

Did my blood flow as riverwater flows
around a tree stump—
crooked, with a lilt?

What other evidence
did I need?

Seventeen Warnings in Search of a Feminist Poem

For Aaron Asher

1   Beware of the man who denounces ambition;
         his fingers itch under his gloves.

2   Beware of the man who denounces war
         through clenched teeth.

3   Beware of the man who denounces women writers;
         his penis is tiny & cannot spell.

4   Beware of the man who wants to protect you;
         he will protect you from everything but himself.

5   Beware of the man who loves to cook;
         he will fill your kitchen with greasy pots.

6   Beware of the man who loves your soul;
         he is a bullshitter.

7   Beware of the man who denounces his mother;
         he is a son of a bitch.

8   Beware of the man who spells son of a bitch as one word;
         he is a hack.

9   Beware of the man who loves death too well;
         he is taking out insurance.

10 Beware of the man who loves life too well;
        he is a fool.

11 Beware of the man who denounces psychiatrists;
        he is afraid.

12 Beware of the man who trusts psychiatrists;
        he is in hock.

13 Beware of the man who picks your dresses;
        he wants to wear them.

14 Beware of the man you think is harmless;
        he will surprise you.

15 Beware of the man who cares for nothing but books;
        he will run like a trickle of ink.

16 Beware of the man who writes flowery love letters;
        he is preparing for years of silence.

17 Beware of the man who praises liberated women;
        he is·planning to quit his job.

Divorce

Eggs boiling in a pot.
They click
like castanets.
I put one in a cup
& slice its head off.

Under the wobbly egg white
is my first husband.
Look how small he's grown
since last we met!

"Eat me," he says agreeably.
I hesitate, then bite.

The thick yolk runs down
my thighs.

I take another egg
& slice its head.
Inside is my second husband.
This one's better done.

"You liked the white," I say,
"I liked the yolk."

He doesn't speak
but scowls as if to say:
"Everyone always eats me
in the end."

I chew him up
but I spit out
his jet-black hair,
the porcelain jackets from his teeth,
his cufflinks, fillings,
eyeglass frames. . . .

I drink my coffee
& I read the *Times*.

Another egg is boiling in the pot.

Paper Cuts

Endless duplication of lives and objects . . .
—Theodore Roethke

I have known the imperial power of secretaries,
the awesome indifference of receptionists,
I have been intimidated by desk & typewriter,
by the silver jaws of the stapler
& the lecherous kiss of the mucilage,
& the unctuousness of rubber cement
before it dries.

I have been afraid of telephones,
have put my mouth to their stale tobacco breath,
have been jarred to terror
by their jangling midnight music,
& their sudden blackness
even when they are white.

I have been afraid in elevators
amid the satin hiss of cables
& the silky lisping of air conditioners
& the helicopter blades of fans.
I have seen time killed in the office jungles
of undeclared war.

My fear has crept into the paper guillotine
& voyaged to the Arctic Circle of the water cooler.

My fear has followed me into the locked Ladies Room,
& down the iron fire stairs
to the postage meter.

I have seen the mailroom women like lost letters
frayed around the edges.
I have seen the Xerox room men
shuffling in & out among each other
like cards in identical decks.

I have come to tell you I have survived.
I bring you chains of paperclips instead of emeralds.
I bring you lottery tickets instead of poems.
I bring you mucilage instead of love.

I lay my body out before you on the desk.
I spread my hair amid a maze of rubber stamps.
RUSH. SPECIAL DELIVERY. DO NOT BEND.
I am open—will you lick me like an envelope?
I am bleeding—will you kiss my paper cuts?

Alcestis on the Poetry Circuit

*(In Memoriam Marina Tsvetayeva, Anna
Wickham, Sylvia Plath, Shakespeare's
sister, etc., etc.)*

The best slave
does not need to be beaten.
She beats herself.

Not with a leather whip,
or with stick or twigs,
not with a blackjack
or a billyclub,
but with the fine whip
of her own tongue
& the subtle beating
of her mind
against her mind.

For who can hate her half so well
as she hates herself?
& who can match the finesse
of her self-abuse?

Years of training
are required for this.
Twenty years
of subtle self-indulgence,

self-denial;
until the subject
thinks herself a queen
& yet a beggar—
both at the same time.
She must doubt herself
in everything but love.

She must choose passionately
& badly.
She must feel lost as a dog
without her master.
She must refer all moral questions
to her mirror.
She must fall in love with a cossack
or a poet.

She must never go out of the house
unless veiled in paint.
She must wear tight shoes
so she always remembers her bondage.
She must never forget
she is rooted in the ground.

Though she is quick to learn
& admittedly clever,
her natural doubt of herself
should make her so weak
that she dabbles brilliantly
in half a dozen talents
& thus embellishes
but does not change
our life.

If she's an artist
& comes close to genius,
the very fact of her gift

should cause her such pain
that she will take her own life
rather than best us.

& after she dies, we will cry
& make her a saint.

Mother

Ash falls on the roof
of my house.

I have cursed you enough
in the lines of my poems
& between them,
in the silences which fall
like ash-flakes
on the watertank
from a smog-bound sky.

I have cursed you
because I remember
the smell of *Joy*
on a sealskin coat
& because I feel
more abandoned than a baby seal
on an ice floe red
with its mother's blood.

I have cursed you
as I walked & prayed
on a concrete terrace
high above the street
because whatever I pulled down
with my bruised hand
from the bruising sky,

whatever lovely plum
came to my mouth
you envied
& spat out.

Because you saw me in your image,
because you favored me,
you punished me.

It was only a form of you
my poems were seeking.
Neither of us knew.

For years
we lived together in a single skin.

We shared fur coats.
We hated each other
as the soul hates the body
for being weak,
as the mind hates the stomach
for needing food,
as one lover hates the other.

I kicked
in the pouch of your theories
like a baby kangaroo.

I believed you
on Marx, on Darwin,
on Tolstoy & Shaw.
I said I loved Pushkin
(you loved him).
I vowed Monet
was better than Bosch.

Who cared?

I would have said nonsense
to please you
& frequently did.

This took the form,
of course,
of fighting you.

We fought so gorgeously!

We fought like one boxer
& his punching bag.
We fought like mismatched twins.
We fought like the secret sharer
& his shade.

Now we're apart.
Time doesn't heal
the baby to the womb.
Separateness is real
& keeps on growing.

One by one the mothers
drop away,
the lovers leave,
the babies outgrow clothes.

Some get insomnia—
the poet's disease—
& sit up nights
nursing
at the nipples
of their pens.

I have made hot milk
& kissed you where you are.
I have cursed my curses.
I have cleared the air.
& now I sit here writing,
breathing you.

The Eggplant Epithalamion

For Grace & David Griffin
& for Iris Love

"Mostly you eat eggplant at least once a day," she explained. "A Turk won't marry a woman unless she can cook eggplant at least a hundred ways."

Archaeologist Iris Love, speaking of the cuisine on digs in Turkey. *The New York Times*, February 4, 1971

1

There are more than a hundred Turkish poems
about eggplant.
I would like to give you all of them.
If you scoop out every seed,
you can read me backward
like an Arabic book.
Look.

2

(Lament in Aubergine)

Oh aubergine,
egg-shaped

& as shiny as if freshly laid—
you are a melancholy fruit.
Solanum Melongena.
Every animal is sad
after eggplant.

3

(Byzantine Eggplant Fable)

Once upon a time on the coast of Turkey
there lived a woman who could cook eggplant 99 ways.
She could slice eggplant thin as paper.
She could write poems on it & batter-fry it.
She could bake eggplant & broil it.
She could even roll the seeds in banana-
flavored cigarette papers
& get her husband high on eggplant.
But he was not pleased.
He went to her father & demanded his bride-price back.
He said he'd been cheated.

He wanted back two goats, twelve chickens
& a camel as reparation.
His wife wept & wept.
Her father raved.

The next day she gave birth to an eggplant.
It was premature & green
& she had to sit on it for days
before it hatched.

"This is my hundredth eggplant recipe," she screamed.
"I hope you're satisfied!"

(Thank Allah that the eggplant was a boy.)

4

(Love & the Eggplant)

On the warm coast of Turkey, Miss Love
eats eggplant
"at least once a day."

How fitting that love should eat eggplant,
that most aphrodisiac fruit.

Fruit of the womb
of Asia Minor,
reminiscent of eggs,
of Istanbul's deep purple nights
& the Byzantine eyes of Christ.

I remember the borders of egg & dart
fencing us off from the flowers & fruit
of antiquity.
I remember the egg & tongue
probing the lost scrolls of love.
I remember the ancient faces
of Aphrodite
hidden by dust
in the labyrinth under
the British Museum
to be finally found by Miss Love
right there
near Great Russell Square.

I think of the hundreds of poems of the eggplant
& my friends who have fallen in love
over an eggplant,
who have opened the eggplant together
& swum in its seeds,
who have clung in the egg of the eggplant
& have rocked to sleep
in love's dark purple boat.

Touch

The house of the body
is a stately manor
open for nothing
never to the public.

But
for the owner of the house,
the key-holder—
the body swings open
like Ali Baba's mountain
glistening with soft gold
& red jewels.

These cannot be stolen
or sold for money.
They only glisten
when the mountain opens
by magic
or its own accord.

The gold triangle of hair,
its gentle *ping,*
the pink quartz crystals
of the skin,
the ruby nipples,
the lapis
of the veins
that swim the breast . . .

The key-holder
is recognized
by the way he holds
the body.
He is recognized
by touch.

Touch is the first sense to awaken
after the body's little death
in sleep.
Touch is the first sense
to alert the raw red infant
to a world of pain.

The body glimmers
on its dark mountain
pretending ignorance of this.

Gardener

I am in love with my womb
& jealous of it.

I cover it tenderly
with a little pink hat
(a sort of yarmulke)
to protect it from men.

Then I listen for the gentle *ping*
of the ovary:
a sort of cupid's bow
released.
I'm proud of that.
& the spot of blood
in the little hat
& the egg so small
I cannot see it
though I pray to it.

I imagine the inside
of my womb to be
the color of poppies
& bougainvillea
(though I've never seen it).

But I fear the barnacle
which might latch on
& not let go

& fear the monster
who might grow
to bite the flowers
& make them swell & bleed.

So I keep my womb empty
& full of possibility.

Each month
the blood sheets down
like good red rain.

I am the gardener.
Nothing grows without me.

The Prisoner

The cage of myself clamps shut.
My words turn the lock.

I am the jailor rattling the keys.
I am the torturer's assistant
who nods & smiles
& pretends not
to be responsible.

I am the clerk who stamps
the death note
affixing the seal, the seal, the seal.

I am the lackey who "follows orders."
I have not got the authority.

I am the visitor
who brings a cake, baked
with a file.

Pale snail,
I wave between the bars.
I speak of rope with the hangman.
I chatter of sparks & currents
with the electrician.
Direct or alternating,
he is beautiful.

I flatter him.
I say he turns me on.

I tell the cyanide capsules
they have talent
& may fulfill themselves someday.
I read the warden's awful novel
& recommend a publisher.
I sleep with the dietitian
who is hungry.
I sleep with the hangman
& reassure him
that he is a good lover.

I am the ideal prisoner.

I win prizes on my conduct.
They reduce my sentence.
Now it is only 99 years
with death like a dollop
of whipped cream at the end.
I am so grateful.

No one remembers
that I constructed this jail
& peopled its cells.
No one remembers my blueprints
& my plans,
my steady hammering,
my dreams of fantastic escapes.

& even I,
patiently writing away,
my skin yellowing
like the pages of old paperbacks,
my hair turning gray,
cannot remember the first crime,
the crime
I was born for.

The Other Side of the Page

I pass to the other side of the page.

—Pablo Neruda

On the other side of the page
where the lost days go,
where the lost poems go,
where the forgotten dreams
breaking up like morning fog
go
go
go

I am preparing myself for death.

I am teaching myself emptiness:
the gambler's hunger for love,
the nun's hunger for God,
the child's hunger for chocolate
in the brown hours
of the dark.

I am teaching myself love:
the lean love of marble
kissed away by rain,
the cold kisses of snow crystals
on granite grave markers,

the soul kisses of snow
as it melts in the spring.

On the other side of the page
I lie making a snow angel
with the arcs
of my arms.

I lie like a fallen skier
who never wants to get up.

I lie with my poles, my pens
flung around me in the snow
too far to reach.

The snow seeps
into the hollows of my bones
& the calcium white of the page
silts me in like a fossil.

I am fixed in my longing for speech,
I am buried in the snowbank of my poems,
I am here where you find me

dead

on the other side of the page.

V

❖

Loveroot

(1975)

To Pablo Neruda

Again & again
I have read your books
without ever wishing to know you.

> I suck the alphabet of blood.
> I chew the iron filings of your words.
> I kiss your images like moist mouths
> while the black seeds of your syllables
> fly, fly, fly
> into my lungs.

Untranslated, untranslatable,
you are rooted inside me—
not you—but the you
of your poems:

> the man of his word,
> the lover who digs into the alien soil
> of one North American woman
> & plants a baby—
> love-child of Whitman
> crossed with the Spanish language,
> embryo, sapling, half-breed
> of my tongue.

◆

I saw you once—
your flesh—
at Columbia.
My alma mater
& you the visiting soul.

Buddha-like
you sat before a Buddha;
& the audience
craned its neck
to take you in.

Freak show—
visiting poet.
You sat clothed
in your thick
imperious flesh.

I wanted to comfort you
& not to stare.
Our words knew each other.
That was enough.

❖

Now you are dead
of fascism & cancer—
your books scattered,
the oil cruet on the floor.

The sea surges through your house
at Isla Negra,
& the jackboots
walk on water.

❖

Poet of cats & grapefruits,
of elephant saints;

170

poet of broken dishes
& Machu Picchu;
poet of panthers
& pantheresses;
poet of lemons,
poet of lemony light.

    The flies swarm
    thicker than print on a page,
    & poetry blackens
    like overripe bananas.
    The fascists you hated,
    the communists you loved,
    obscure the light, the lemons
    with their buzzing.

We were together
on the side of light.
We walked together
though we never met.
    The eyes are not political,
    nor the tastebuds,
    & the flesh tastes salty always
    like the sea;
    & the sea
    turns back the flies.

Dear Colette

Dear Colette,
I want to write to you
about being a woman
for that is what you write to me.

I want to tell you how your face
enduring after thirty, forty, fifty . . .
hangs above my desk
like my own muse.

I want to tell you how your hands
reach out from your books
& seize my heart.

I want to tell you how your hair
electrifies my thoughts
like my own halo.

I want to tell you how your eyes
penetrate my fear
& make it melt.

I want to tell you
simply that I love you—
though you are "dead"
& I am still "alive."

❖

Suicides & spinsters—
all our kind!

Even decorous Jane Austen
never marrying,
& Sappho leaping,
& Sylvia in the oven,
& Anna Wickham, Tsvetaeva, Sara Teasdale,
& pale Virginia floating like Ophelia,
& Emily alone, alone, alone. . . .

But you endure & marry,
go on writing,
lose a husband, gain a husband,
go on writing,
sing & tap dance
& you go on writing,
have a child & still
you go on writing,
love a woman, love a man
& go on writing.
You endure your writing
& your life.

❖

Dear Colette,
I only want to thank you:

for your eyes ringed
with bluest paint like bruises,
for your hair gathering sparks
like brush fire,
for your hands which never willingly
let go,
for your years, your child, your lovers,
all your books. . . .

Dear Colette,
you hold me
to this life.

Dear Marys, Dear Mother, Dear Daughter

Mary Wollstonecraft Godwin
Author of
A Vindication
Of the Rights of Woman:
Born 27 April, 1759:
Died 10 September, 1797
——MARY WOLLSTONECRAFT'S
GRAVESTONE, PLACED BY
WILLIAM GODWIN, 1798

I was lonesome as a Crusoe.
——MARY SHELLEY

It is all over,
little one, the flipping
and overleaping, the watery
somersaulting alone in the oneness
under the hill, under
the old, lonely bellybutton . . .
——GALWAY KINNELL

What terrified me will terrify others . . .
——MARY SHELLEY

1 / Needlepoint

Mothers & daughters . . .
something sharp
catches in my throat
as I watch my mother
nervous before flight,
do needlepoint—
blue irises & yellow daffodils
against a stippled woolen sky.

She pushes the needle
in & out
as she once pushed me:
sharp needle to the canvas of her life—
embroidering her faults
in prose & poetry,
writing the fiction
of my bitterness,
the poems of my need.

"You hate me," she accuses,
needle poised,
"why not admit it?"

I shake my head.
The air is thick
with love gone bad,
the odor of old blood.

If I were small enough
I would suck your breast . .
but I say nothing,
big mouth,
filled with poems.

Whatever love is made of—
wool, blood, Sunday lamb,
books of verse
with violets crushed
between the pages,
tea with herbs,
lemon juice for hair,
portraits sketched of me asleep
at nine months old—
this twisted skein
of multicolored wool,
this dappled canvas
or this page of print
joins us
like the twisted purple cord
through which we first pulsed poems.

Mother, what I feel for you
is more
& less
than love.

2 | *Mary Wollstonecraft Godwin & Mary Godwin Shelley*

She was "lonesome
as a Crusoe,"
orphaned by childbirth,
orphaned being born,
killing her mother
with a stubborn afterbirth—
the medium they'd shared. . . .

Puppies were brought
to draw off Mary's milk,
& baby Mary screamed.

She grew up
to marry Shelley,

have four babes
(of whom three died)—
& one immortal monster.

Byron & Shelley
strutted near the lake
& wrote their poems
on purest alpine air.
The women had their pregnancies
& fears.

They bore the babies,
copied manuscripts,
& listened to the talk
that love was "free."

The brotherhood of man
did not apply:
all they contributed
to life
was life.

& Doctor Frankenstein
was punished
for his pride:
the hubris of a man
creating life.
He reared a wretched
animated corpse—
& Shelley praised the book
but missed the point.

Who were these gothic monsters?
Merely men.
Self-exiled Byron
with his Mistress Fame,
& Percy Shelley
with his brains aboil,

the seaman
who had never learned to swim.

Dear Marys,
it was clear
that you were truer.
Daughters of daughters,
mothers of future mothers,
you sought to soar
beyond complaints
of woman's lot—
& died in childbirth
for the Rights of Man.

3 | Exiles

This was the sharpness
of my mother's lesson.
Being a woman
meant eternal strife.
No colored wool could stitch
the trouble up;
no needlepoint
could cover it with flowers.

When Byron played
the exiled wanderer,
he left his ladies
pregnant or in ruin.
He left his children
fatherless for fame,
then wrote great letters
theorizing pain.

He scarcely knew
his daughters any more
than Mary knew the Mary

who expired
giving her birth.

All that remained in him:
a hollow loneliness
about the heart,
the milkless tug of memory,
the singleness of creatures
who breathe air.

Birth is the start
of loneliness
& loneliness the start
of poetry:
that seems a crude
reduction of it all,
but truth
is often crude.

& so I dream
of daughters
as a man might dream
of giving birth,
& as my mother dreamed
of daughters
& had three—
none of them her dream.

& I reach out for love
to other women
while my real mother
pines for me
& I pine for her,
knowing I would have to be
smaller than a needle
pierced with wool
to pierce the canvas of her life
again.

4 / Dear Daughter

Will you change all this
by my having you,
& by your having everything—
Don Juan's exuberance,
Childe Harold's pilgrimage,
books & babies,
recipes & riots?

Probably not.

In making daughters
there is so much needlepoint,
so much doing & undoing,
so much yearning—
that the finished pattern cannot please.

My poems will have daughters
everywhere,
but my own daughter
will have to grow
into her energy.

I will not call her Mary
or Erica.
She will shape
a wholly separate name.

& if her finger falters
on the needle,
& if she ever needs to say
she hates me,
& if she loathes poetry
& loves to whistle,
& if she never
calls me Mother,
She will always be my daughter—

my filament of soul
that flew,
& caught.

She will come
in a radiance of new-made skin,
in a room of dying men
and dying flowers,
in the shadow of her large mother,
with her books propped up
& her ink-stained fingers,
lying back on pillows
white as blank pages,
laughing—
"I did it without
words!"

Elegy for a Whale

*Francis, the only pregnant white whale in
captivity, died last night of internal
poisoning in her tank at the New York
Aquarium at Coney Island. . . .*

    —The New York Times, May 26, 1974

Too big & too intelligent
to reproduce,
the ferns will outlast us,
not needing each other
with their dark spores,
& the cockroaches
with their millions of egg-cases,
& even the one-celled waltzers
dancing pseudopod to pseudopod,
but we are too big, too smart
to stick around.

Floating in Coney Island,
floating on her white belly—
while the fetus flips its flippers
in the womb
& she circles in the belly of the tank.

The last calf
beat her brains out
minutes after birth
& this one died unborn . . .

Fourteen months in the womb,
fourteen months to enter
the world of whaledom
through a tank in Coney Island.
Not worth it,
the calf decides,
& dies,
taking along its mother.

❖

The whales are friendly, social animals,
& produce big, brainy babies;
produce them one by one
in the deep arctic waters,
produce them painfully
through months of mating
& pregnancies that last more than a year.

They croon to their unborn calves
in poetry—whale poetry
which only a few humans
have been privileged to hear.
Melville died for the privilege
& so will I
straining my ears
all the way to Coney Island.

❖

Dear Francis, dead at ten
in your second pregnancy,
in the seventh year of captivity . . .
Was it weariness of the tank, the cage,
the zoo-prison of marriage?
Or was it loneliness—
the loneliness of pregnant whales?

Or was it nostalgia for the womb,
the arctic waste,
the belly of your own cold mother?

When a whale dies at sixteen hundred pounds
we must make big moans.
When a whale dies with an unborn baby
of one hundred and fifty pounds—
a small elegy is not enough;
we must weep loud enough
to be heard
all the way to Coney Island.

◆

Why am I weeping
into *The New York Times*
for a big beluga whale
who could never have been
my sister?

Why am I weeping for a baby whale
who died happy
in the confines of the womb?

Because when the big-brained babies
die, we are all dying;
& the ferns live on
shivering
in the warm wind.

For My Sister, Against Narrowness

Narrowing life because of the fears,
narrowing it between the dust motes,
narrowing the pink baby
between the green-limbed monsters,
& the drooling idiots,
& the ghosts of Thalidomide infants,
narrowing hope,
always narrowing hope.

Mother sits on one shoulder hissing:
Life is dangerous.
Father sits on the other sighing:
Lucky you.
Grandmother, grandfather, big sister:
You'll die if you leave us,
you'll die if you ever leave us.

Sweetheart, baby sister,
you'll die anyway
& so will I.
Even if you walk the wide greensward,
even if you
& your beautiful big belly
embrace the world of men & trees,
even if you moan with pleasure,
& smoke the sweet grass
& feast on strawberries in bed,
you'll die anyway—

wide or narrow,
you're going to die.

As long as you're at it,
die wide.
Follow your belly to the green pasture.
Lie down in the sun's dapple.
Life is not as dangerous
as mother said.
It is more dangerous,
more wide.

For My Husband

You sleep in the darkness,
you with the back I love
& the gift of sleeping
through my noisy nights of poetry.

I have taken other men into my thoughts
since I met you.
I have loved parts of them.
But only you sleep on through the darkness
like a mountain where my house is planted,
like a rock on which my temple stands,
like a great dictionary holding every word—
even some
I have never spoken.

You breathe.
The pages of your dreams are riffled
by the winds of my writing.
The pillow creases your cheek
as I cover pages.

Element in which I swim
or fly,
silent muse, backbone, companion—
it is unfashionable
to confess to marriage—
yet I feel no bondage
in this air we share.

Cheever's People

These beautifully grown men. These hungerers.
Look at them looking!
They're overdrawn on all accounts but hope
& they've missed
(for the hundredth time) the express
to the city of dreams
& settled, sighing, for a desperate local;
so who's to blame them
if they swim through swimming pools of twelve-
year-old scotch, or fall
in love with widows (other than their wives)
who suddenly can't ride
in elevators? In that suburb of elms
& crabgrass (to which
the angel banished them) nothing is more real
than last night's empties.

So, if they pack up, stuff their vitals
in a two-suiter,
& (with passports bluer than their eyes)
pose as barons
in Kitzbühel, or poets in Portofino,
something in us sails
off with them (dreaming of bacon-lettuce-
and-tomato sandwiches).
Oh, all the exiles of the twenties knew
that America
was discovered this way: desperate men,

wearing nostalgia
like a hangover, sailed out, sailed out
in search of passports,
eyes, an ancient kingdom, beyond the absurd
suburbs of the heart.

Dear Anne Sexton, I

On line at the supermarket
waiting for the tally,
the blue numerals
tattooed
on the white skins
of paper,
I read your open book
of folly
and take heart,
poet of my heart.

The poet as housewife!
Keeper of steak & liver,
keeper of keys, locks, razors,
keeper of blood & apples,
of breasts & angels,
Jesus & beautiful women,
keeper also of women
who are not beautiful—

you glide in from Cape Ann
on your winged broomstick—
the housewife's Pegasus.

You are sweeping the skies clear
of celestial rubbish.
You are placing a child there,
a heart here . . .
You are singing for your supper.

191

Dearest wordmother & hunger-teacher,
full professor of courage,
dean of women
in my school of books,
thank you.

I have checked out
pounds of meat & cans of soup.
I walk home laden,
light with writing you.

Dear Anne Sexton, II

My dearest Anne,
I am living by a lake
with a young man
I met one week after you died.

His beard is red,
his eyes flicker like cat's eyes,
& the amazing plum of his tongue
sweetens my brain.
He is like nobody
since I love him.
His cock sinks deep
in my heart.

❖

I have owed you a letter
for months.

❖

I wanted to chide
the manner of your death
the way I might have once
revised your poem.
You are like nobody
since I love you,
& you are gone.

❖

Can you believe
your death gave birth to me?
Live or die,
you said insistently.
You chose the second
& the first chose me.
I mourned you
& I found him
in one week.

❖

Is love the sugar-coated poison
that gets us in the end?
We spoke of men
as often as of poems.
We tried to legislate away
the need for love—
that backseat fuck
& death caressing you.

❖

Why did you do it
in your mother's coat?
(I know
but also know
I have to ask.)
Our mothers get us hooked,
then leave us cold,
all full-grown orphans
hungering after love.

❖

You loved a man who spoke
"like greeting cards."
"He fucks me well
but I can't talk to him."

We shared that awful need
to talk in bed.
Love wasn't love
if we could only speak
in tongues.

❖

& the intensity of unlove
increased
until the motor, the running motor
could no longer power
the driver,
& you, with miles to go,
would rather sleep.

❖

Between the pills, the suicide pills
& our giggly vodkas in the Algonquin . . .
Between your round granny glasses
& your eyes blue as glaciers . . .
Between your stark mother-hunger
& your mother courage,
you knew there was only one poem
we all were writing.

❖

No competition.
"The poem belongs to everyone
& God."
I jumped out of your
suicide car
& into his arms.

Your death was mine.
I ate it
& returned.

❖

Now I sit by a lake
writing to you.
I love a man
who makes my fingers ache.
I type to you
off somewhere in the clouds.
I tap the table
like a spiritualist.

❖

Sex is a part of death;
that much I know.
Your voice was earth,
your eyes were glacier-blue.
Your slender torso
& long-stemmed American legs
drape across
this huge blue western sky.

❖

I want to tell you "Wait,
don't do it yet."
Love is the poison, Anne,
but love eats death.

Dearest Man-in-the-Moon,

ever since our lunch of cheese
& moonjuice
on the far side of the sun,
I have walked the craters of New York,
a trail of slime
ribboning between my legs,
a phosphorescent banner
which is tied to you,
a beam of moonlight
focused on your navel,
a silver chain
from which my body dangles,
& my whole torso chiming
like sleighbells in a Russian novel.

Dearest man-in-the moon,
I used to fear moonlight
thinking her my mother.
I used to dread nights
when the moon was full.
I used to scream
"Pull down the shade!"
because the moonface leered at me,
because I felt her mocking,
because my fear lived in me
like rats in a wheel of cheese.

You have eaten out my fear.
You have licked
the creamy inside of my moon.
You have kissed
the final crescent of my heart
& made it full.

Dear Keats

For Howard Moss

Already six years past your age!
The steps in Rome,
the house near Hampstead Heath,
& all your fears
that you might cease to be
before your pen had glean'd. . . .

My dear dead friend,
you were the first to teach me
how the dust could sing.
I followed in your footsteps
up the Heath.
I listened hard
for Lethe's nightingale.

& now at 31, I want to live.
Oblivion holds no adolescent charms.
& all the "souls of poets
dead & gone,"
& all the "Bards
of Passion & Mirth"
cannot make death—
its echo, its damp earth—
resemble birth.

❖

You died in Rome—
in faltering sunlight—
Bernini's watery boat still sinking
in the fountain in the square below.
When Severn came to say
the roses bloomed,
you did not "glut thy sorrow,"
but you wept—
you wept for them
& for your posthumous life.

& yet we all lead posthumous lives somehow.
The broken lyre,
the broken lung,
the broken love.
Our names are writ in newsprint
if not water.

"Don't breathe on me—" you cried,
"it comes like ice."

❖

Last words.
(I can't imagine mine.
Perhaps some muttered dream,
some poem, some curse.)

Three months past 25,
you lived on milk.
They reeled you backward
in the womb of love.

❖

A tepid February Roman Spring.
Fruit trees in bloom
& Hampstead still in snow
& Fanny Brawne receives a hopeful note
when you are two weeks dead.

200

A poet's life:
always awaiting mail.

◆

For God's sake
kick against the pricks!
There aren't very many roses.
Your life was like an hourglass
with no sand.
The words slid through
& rested under glass;
the flesh decayed
to moist Italian clay.

◆

At autopsy,
your lungs were wholly gone.
Was that from too much singing?
Too many rifts of ore?
You spent your life breath
breathing life in words.
But words return no breath
to those who write.

Letters, Life, & Literary Remains . . .

"I find that I cannot exist without poetry. . . ."

"O for a Life of Sensations rather than of Thoughts!"

"What the imagination seizes as Beauty must be truth. . . ."

"We hate poetry that has a palpable design upon us. . . ."

"Sancho will invent a Journey heavenwards as well as anybody. . . ."

"Poetry should be great and unobtrusive, a thing which enters into
one's soul."

"Why should we kick against the Pricks when we can walk on Roses?"

"Axioms in philosophy are not axioms until they are proved upon our pulses. . . ."

"Until we are sick, we understand not. . . ."

"Sorrow is Wisdom. . . ."

"Wisdom is folly. . . ."

❖

Too wise
& yet not wise enough
at 25.
Sick, you understood
& understanding
were too weak to write.

Proved on the pulse: poetry.

If sorrow is wisdom
& wisdom is folly
then too much sorrow
is folly.

I find that I cannot exist without sorrow
& I find that sorrow
cannot exist without poetry. . . .

What the imagination seizes as beauty
must be poetry. . . .

What the imagination seizes must be. . .

❖

You claimed no lust for fame
& yet you burned.

"The faint conceptions I have of poems to come brings
the blood frequently into my forehead."

I burn like you
until it often seems
my blood will break
the boundaries of my brain
& issue forth in one tall fountain
from my skull.

❖

A spume of blood from the forehead: poetry.

A plume of blood from the heart: poetry.

Blood from the lungs: alizarin crimson words.

❖

"I will not spoil my love of gloom
by writing an Ode to Darkness. . . ."

The blood turns dark;
it stiffens on the sheet.
At night the childhood walls
are streaked with blood—
until the darkness seems awash with red
& children sleep behind two blood-branched lids.

❖

"My imagination is a monastery
& I am its monk . . ."

At five & twenty,
very far from home,
death picked you up
& sorted to a pip.
& 15 decades later,

your words breathe:
syllables of blood.

A strange transfusion
for my feverish verse.

I suck your breath,
your rhythms & your blood,
& all my fiercest dreams are sighed away.

I send you love,
dear Keats,
I send you peace.
Since flesh can't stay
we keep the breath aloft.

Since flesh can't stay,
we pass the words along.

Becoming a Nun

For Jennifer Josephy

On cold days
it is easy to be reasonable,
to button the mouth against kisses,
dust the breasts
with talcum powder
& forget
the red pulp meat
of the heart.

On those days
it beats
like a digital clock—
not a beat at all
but a steady whirring
chilly as green neon,
luminous as numerals in the dark,
cool as electricity.

& I think:
I can live without it all—
love with its blood pump,
sex with its messy hungers,
men with their peacock strutting,
their silly sexual baggage,
their wet tongues in my ear

& their words like little sugar suckers
with sour centers.

On such days
I am zipped in my body suit,
I am wearing seven league red suede boots,
I am marching over the cobblestones
as if they were the heads of men,

& I am happy
as a seven-year-old virgin
holding Daddy's hand.

Don't touch.
Don't try to tempt me with your ripe persimmons.
Don't threaten me with your volcano.
The sky is clearer when I'm not in heat,
& the poems
are colder.

Empty

. . . *who shall measure the heat and
violence of the poet's heart when caught
and tangled in a woman's body?*

—Virginia Woolf

Every month,
the reminder of emptiness
so that you are tuned
to your bodyharp,
strung out on the harpsichord
of all your nerves
& hammered bloody blue
as the crushed fingers
of the woman pianist
beaten by her jealous lover.

Who was she?
Someone I invented
for this poem,
someone I imagined . . .

Never mind,
she is me, you—

tied to that bodybeat,
fainting on the rack of blood,
moving to the metronome—
empty, empty, empty.

No use.
The blood is thicker
than the roots of trees,
more persistent than my poetry,
more baroque than her bruised music.
It gilds the sky above the Virgin's head.
It turns the lilies white.

Try to run:
the blood still follows you.
Swear off children,
seek a quiet room
to practice your preludes & fugues.
Under the piano,
the blood accumulates;
eventually it floats you both away.

Give in.
Babies cry & music is your life.
Darling, you were born to bleed
or rock.
& the heart breaks
either way.

Egyptology

I am the Sphinx.
I am the woman buried in sand
up to her chin.
I am waiting for an archaeologist
to unearth me,
to dig out my neck & my nipples,
bare my claws
& solve my riddle.

No one has solved my riddle
since Oedipus.

♦

I face the pyramids which rise
like angular breasts
from the dry body of Egypt.
My fertile river is flowing down below—
a lovely lower kingdom.
Every woman should have a delta
with such rich silt—
brown as the buttocks
of Nubian queens.

♦

O friend, why have you come to Egypt?
Aton & Yahweh
are still feuding.
Moses is leading his people

& speaking of guilt.
The voice out of the volcano
will not be still.

❖

A religion of death,
a woman buried alive.
For thousands of years
the sand drifted over my head.
My sex was a desert,
my hair more porous than pumice,
& nobody sucked my lips
to make me tell.

❖

The pyramid breasts, though huge,
will never sag.
In the center of each one,
a king lies buried.
In the center of each one,
a darkened chamber . . .
a tunnel,
dead men's bones,
malignant gold.

Parable of the Four-Poster

Because she wants to touch him,
she moves away.
Because she wants to talk to him,
she keeps silent.
Because she wants to kiss him,
she turns away
& kisses a man she does not want to kiss.

He watches
thinking she does not want him.
He listens
hearing her silence.
He turns away
thinking her distant
& kisses a girl he does not want to kiss.

They marry each other—
a four-way mistake.
He goes to bed with his wife
thinking of her.
She goes to bed with her husband
thinking of him.
—& all this in a real old-fashioned four-poster bed.

Do they live unhappily ever after?
Of course.
Do they undo their mistakes ever?

Never.
Who is the victim here?
Love is the victim.
Who is the villain?
Love that never dies.

Tapestry, with Unicorn

What we were searching for
did not, of course, exist—
that tapestried morning,
under those woven clouds
where impossible birds
sang quite incredibly
of unattainable things.

A moth among the dandelions
warbled like the nightingale of Keats,
& trochees sang among the iambs,
while you in your curled collar & brocaded vest,
were beaming down the sun-strewn silken grass
where I lay in a frenzy of ruffles,
ear pressed to the earth
so I might hear—
the echoing hoofbeats of the unicorn.

He came in a blaze
of embroidered glory, with agate eyes
and his infamous ivory horn
blaring baroque concerti—
& thinking to have captured him for good,
we toasted in white wine and wafers,
and took before witnesses,
impossible vows.

The rest you know:
how in the toadstool damp of evening
where lovers toss and cough,
speaking to each other
in the thick syllables of sleep,
through the long winter's night of marriage,
the unicorn slips away,
& love, like an insomniac's nightmare,
becomes only
the lesser of two evils.

Sometimes he comes again,
thrashing through the tapestried dark,
uprooting limbs & sheets
& finespun wisps of hair.
But the quest having been forgotten,
we do not know him,
or else we call him
by a different name.

The Poet Writes in *I*

The poet writes in *I*
because she knows
no other language.

We is a continent,
& a poet must be
an island.

She is an inlet.
He is a peninsula.
They is the great engulfing sea.

The poet writes in *I*
as the clock
strikes on metal,

as the bee wing
flies on honey,
as trees are rooted
in the sky.

I is the language
of the poet's inner chantings:
a geography of sadness,

a metronome of pain,
a map of elevations
in the jungled heart.

Sunjuice

What happens when the juice of the sun
drenches you
with its lemony tang, its tart sweetness
& your whole body stings with singing
so that your toes sing to your mouth
& your navel whistles to your breasts
& your breasts wave to everyone
as you walk down the summer street?

What will you do
when nothing will do
but to throw your arms around trees
& men
& greet every woman as sister
& to run naked in the spray of the fire hydrants
with children of assorted colors?

Will you cover your drenched skin
with woolen clothes?
Will you wear a diaper of herringbone tweed?
Will you piece together a shroud of figleaves
& lecture at the University
on the Lives of the Major Poets,
the History of Despair in Art?

Insomnia & Poetry

Sweet muse
with bitter milk,
I have lain
between your breasts,
put my ear
to your sea-shell-whispering navel,
& strained the salty marshes
of your sex
between my milk teeth.
Then I've slept at last,
my teeming head
against your rocking thigh.

Gentle angry mother
poetry,
where could I turn
from the terror of the night
but to your sweet maddening
ambivalence?
Where could I rest
but in your hurricane?
Who would always take me home
but you,
sweeping off the sooty stoop
of your wind-filled shack
on the edge
of the volcano?

VI

❖

FROM

How to Save Your Own Life
(1977)

The Puzzle

They locked into each other
like brother & sister,
long-lost relations,
orphans divided by time.

He bit her shoulder
& entered her blood forever.
She bit his tongue
& changed the tone of his song.

They walked together astonished
not to be lonely.
They sought their lonelinesses
like lost dogs.

But they were joined together
by tongue & shoulder.
His nightmares woke her;
her daydreams startled him.

He fucked so hard
he thought he'd climb back in her.
She came so hard
her skin seemed to dissolve.

She feared she had no yearning
left to write with.
He feared she'd suck him dry
& glide away.

They spoke of all these things
& locked together.
She figured out
the jigsaw of his heart.

& he unscrambled her
& placed the pieces
with such precision
nothing came apart.

The Long Tunnel of Wanting You

This is the long tunnel of wanting you.
Its walls are lined with remembered kisses
wet & red as the inside of your mouth,
full & juicy as your probing tongue,
warm as your belly against mine,
deep as your navel leading home,
soft as your sleeping cock beginning to stir,
tight as your legs wrapped around mine,
straight as your toes pointing toward the bed
as you roll over & thrust your hardness
into the long tunnel of my wanting,
seeding it with dreams & unbearable hope,
making memories of the future,
straightening out my crooked past,
teaching me to live in the present present tense
with the past perfect and the uncertain future
suddenly certain for certain
in the long tunnel of my old wanting
which before always had an ending
but now begins & begins again
with you, with you, with you.

The Muse Who Came to Stay

You are the first muse who came to stay.
The others began & ended with a wish,
or a glance or a kiss between stanzas;
the others strode away in the pointed boots of their fear

or were kicked out by the stiletto heels of mine,
or merely padded away in bare feet
when the ground was too hard or cold
or as hot as white sand baked under the noonday sun.

But you flew in on the wings of your smile,
powered by the engine of your cock,
driven by your lonely pumping heart,
rooted by your arteries to mine.

We became a tree with a double apical point,
reaching equally toward what some call heaven,
singing in the wind with our branches,
sharing the sap & syrup
which makes the trunk grow thick.

We are seeding the ground with poems & children.
We are the stuff of books & new-grown forests.
We are renewing the earth with our roots,
the air with our pure oxygen songs,
the nearby seas with leaves we lose
only to grow the greener ones again.

I used to leap from tree to tree,
speaking glibly of Druids,
thinking myself a latter-day dryad,
or a wood nymph from the stony city,
or some other chimerical creature,
conjured in my cheating poet's heart.

But now I stay, knowing the muse is mine,
knowing no books will banish him
& no off-key songs will drive him away.

I being & begin; I whistle in & out of tune.
If the ending is near, I do not think of it.
If the drought comes, we will make our own rain.
If the muse is grounded, I will make him fly,
& if he falls, I will catch him in my arms
until he flies with me again.

We Learned

the decorum of fire . . .

---Pablo Neruda

We learned the decorum of fire,
the flame's curious symmetry,
the blue heat at the center of the thighs,
the flickering red of the hips,
& the tallow gold of the breasts
lit from within
by the lantern in the ribs.

You tear yourself out of me
like a branch that longs to be grafted
onto a fruit tree,
peach & pear
crossed with each other,
fig & banana served on one plate,
the leaf & the luminous snail
that clings to it.

We learned that the tearing
could be a joining,
that the fire's flickering
could be a kindling,
that the old decorum of love—
to die into the poem,
leaving the lover lonely with her pen—
was all an ancient lie.

So we banished the evil eye:
you have to be unhappy to create;
you have to let love die before it writes;
you have to lose the joy to have the poem—
& we re-wrote our lives with fire.

See this manuscript covered
with flesh-colored words?
It was written in invisible ink
& held up to our flame.

The words darkened on the page
as we sank into each other.

We are ink & blood
& all things that make stains.
We turn each other golden as we turn,
browning each other's skins like suns.

Hold me up to the light;
you will see poems.

Hold me in the dark;
you will see light.

Doubts Before Dreaming

Contending with the demon doubt
when all of life heaves up into your mouth,
the lies you spat back with your mother's milk,
the men you loved & hated & betrayed,
the husbands who slept on through windy nights,
the rattling at the panes . . .

Pain, doubt, the ache to love again.
The man you cuddled to your chest
who went away . . .
The demon doubt comes back to haunt your life.
You chose to live, & choosing life meant pain.

❖

Throw out the generalizations!
What you meant—you liar poet—
lyre in your mouth . . .
You meant: I loved him once
& can no more.
You meant: I kept confusing guilt with love.

❖

This is the problem: that we live;
& as we live each body cell must change.
We dream, & as we dream our dreams must change.
We eat, & in devouring life, we change.

❖

We dream we read our lives in some huge book.
Our dreaming eyelids flick the pages past.
The muse writes through our dreams
& dreams our lives.
The book has pages torn & broken type.

❖

& as we dream, some paragraphs are blurred.
& as we read we re-invent the plot.
The eyes are dreaming cells, the eyelids move.
The cells divide as lovers fall apart.

❖

They slide away to sleep, he slips from her.
He sinks into her dream, her dream is filled.
& as she fills with him, her eyes are changed.
He dreams a woman he has never met.

❖

Nothing can stay: the cock grows soft by dawn.
& she seals over like a virgin raped only by dreams.
However much they cling, they drift apart.
Their hands are joined, their dreaming hearts are severed.

❖

They dance the dance of dreamers as they sleep.
This dreamers' dance: the pattern of their lives.
The partners change, yet always stay the same.
The partners bow, their hearts collide & break.

❖

Slippers beneath the bed, bare toes toward heaven.
Soles cradled in the sheet, the dancers sleep.
They dream they dance & dance & dance again.
They dream the dance of dreamers without feet.

❖

What is the question here? I cannot say.
I am asleep, my tongue is blurred by death.
I spit the pits of death across the bed.
I love my love, yet eat him while he sleeps.

❖

Death is confusing, life more confusing still.
Alive, we dream, & dead, who can be sure?
Since all we have are dreams, let's join our beds.

The Dirty Laundry Poem

This is the dirty laundry poem——
because we have traveled from town to town
accumulating soiled linen & sweaty shirts
& blue-jeans caked & clotted with our juice
& teeshirts crumpled by our gloriously messy passion
& underwear made stiff by all our joy.

I have come home to wash my clothes.
They patter on the bathroom floor like rain.
The water drips away the days till you.
The dirty water speaks to me of love.

Steamy in the bubbles of our love,
I have plunged my hands into hot water
as I might plunge them
in your heart.

After years of spots & splatters,
I am finally coming clean.
I will fly to you with a suitcase of fresh laundry,
strip my clothes off, heap them on the floor,
& let you scrub my body with your love.

Sailing Home

In the redwood house sailing off
into the ocean,
I sleep with you—
our dreams mingling,
our breath coming & going
like gusts of wind
trifling with the breakers,
our arms touching
& our legs & our hair
reaching out like tendrils
to intertwine.

The first time
I slept in your arms,
I knew I had come home.
Your body was a ship
& I rocked in it,
utterly safe in the breakers,
utterly sure of this love.
I fit into your arms
as a ship fits into water,
as a cactus roots in sand,
as the sun nestles into the blazing horizon.

The house sails all night.
Our dreams are the flags
of little ships,
your penis the mast

of one of the breeziest sailboats,
& my breasts floating,
half in & half out
of the water,
are like messages in bottles.

There is no point to this poem.
What the sea loses
always turns up again;
it is only a question of shores.

Living Happily Ever After

We used to strike sparks
off each other.
Our eyes would meet
or our hands,
& the blue lightning of love
would sear the air.

Now we are soft.
We loll
in the same sleepy bed,
skin of my skin,
hair of my head,
sweat of my sweat—
you are kin,
brother & mother
all in one,
husband, lover, muse & comforter;
I love you even better
without sparks.

We are pebbles in the tide
rolling against each other.
The surf crashes above us;
the irregular pulse
of the ocean drives our blood,
but we are growing smooth
against each other.

Are we living happily ever after?
What will happen
to my love of cataclysms?
My love of sparks & fire,
my love of ice?

Fellow pebble,
let us roll
against each other.
Perhaps the sparks are clearer
under water.

The Surgery of the Sea

At the furthermost reach of the sea
where Atlantis sinks under the wake of the waves,
I have come to heal my life.

I knit together like a broken arm.
The salt fills in the crevices of bone.
The sea takes all the fragments of my lives
& grinds them home.

I wake up in a waterbed with you.
The sea is singing & my skin
sings against your skin.
The waves are all around us & within.
We sleep stuck to each other's salt.

I am healing in your arms.
I am learning to write without the loss of love.
I am growing deeper lungs here by the sea.
The waves are knives; they glitter & cut clean.

This is the sea's surgery.
This is the cutting & the healing both.
This is where bright sunlight warms the bone,
& fog erases us, then makes us whole.

After the Earthquake

After the first astounding rush,
after the weeks at the lake,
the crystal, the clouds, the water lapping the rocks,
the snow breaking under our boots like skin,
& the long mornings in bed . . .

After the tangos in the kitchen,
& our eyes fixed on each other at dinner,
as if we would eat with our lids,
as if we would swallow each other . . .

I find you still
here beside me in bed,
(while my pen scratches the pad
& your skin glows as you read)
& my whole life so mellowed & changed

that at times I cannot remember
the crimp in my heart that brought me to you,
the pain of a marriage like an old ache,
a husband like an arthritic knuckle.

Here, living with you,
love is still the only subject that matters.
I open to you like a flowering wound,
or a trough in the sea filled with dreaming fish,
or a steaming chasm of earth
split by a major quake.

You changed the topography.
Where valleys were,
there now are mountains.
Where deserts were,
there now are seas.

We rub each other,
but we do not wear away.

The sand gets finer
& our skins turn silk.

VII

❖

Witches

(1981)

To the Goddess

Goddess, I come to you
my neck wreathed with rosebuds,
my head filled with visions of infants,
my eyes open to your rays of illumination,
my palms open to your silver nails,
my vagina & my womb gaping
to be filled by your radiance . . .
O goddess, I would be a worthy vessel.

Impermanence—all is impermanence.
The cock rises to fall again;
the woman fills only to empty
in a convulsion that shakes the world;
the poet grows to become a voice
only to lose that voice when death takes her.
A stroke cancels her upon the page—
& yet I open her book & a chill wind blows from eternity.

Goddess, I come to you
wreathed in tears, in losses, in whistling winds.
I wrap the witch's herbs around my neck
to ward off the impermanence that is our common fate.
The herbs dry & crumble,
as my face grows the map of my anxieties,
& my daughter leaps up like a vine
twining around the trellis of impermanence.

O goddess, teach me to praise loss,
death & the passing of all things—for from this flux
I know your blessings flow.

To the Horned God

The extinct stars
look down
on the centuries
of the horned God.

From the dark recesses
of the Caverne
des Trois Frères
in Ariège,
to the horned Moses
of Michelangelo,
in Rome,
from the Bull of Minos
& his leaping dancers
poised on the horns
of the dilemma . . .

From Pan
laughing & fucking
& making light
of all devils,

to the Devil himself,
the Man in Black,
conjured by
the lusts of Christians . . .

From Osiris
of the upper &

lower kingdoms,
to the Minotaur of azure Crete
& his lost labyrinth . . .

From Cernunnos
to Satan—
God of dark desires—
what a decline
in horny Gods!

O for a goat to dance with!
O for a circle of witches
skyclad under the horned moon!

Outside my window
hunters are shooting deer.
Thus has your worship sunk.

O God with horns,
come back.
O unicorn in captivity,
come lead us out
of our willful darkness!

Come skewer the sun
with your pointed horns,
& make the cave,
the skull, the pelvic arch
once more
a place of light.

Figure of the Witch

Witch-woman,
tall, slender,
Circe at her loom
or murderous Medea,
Joan at her tree,
listening to voices
in the rustling of the leaves,
like the rustling of the flames
which ignited
her deciduous life . . .

Witch-woman,
burning goddess,
every woman bears
within her soul
the figure of the witch,
the face of the witch,
beautiful & hideous,
hidden as the lips
of her cunt,
open as her open eyes,
which see the fire
without screaming

as she & the tree, her mother,
are joined again,
seared,
united,

married as a forest
marries air,
only by its burning,
only by its rising
in Demeter's flaming hands,
only by its leaping

heavenward

in a single
green
flame.

Baby-Witch

Baby-witch,
my daughter,
my worship of the Goddess
alone
condemns you to the fire . . .

I blow upon
your least fingernail
& it flares cyclamen & rose.
I suck flames from your ears.
I touch your perfect nostrils
& they, too, flame gently
like that pale rose
called "sweetheart."

Your eyelids are tender purple
like the base of the flame
before it blues.

O child of fire,
O tiny devotee of the Goddess—

I wished for you
to be born a daughter
though we know

246

that daughters
cannot but be

born for burning
like the fatal
tree.

How to Name Your Familiar

When the devil brings him,
like a Christmas puppy,
examine his downy fur & smell
his small paws for the scent
of sulphur.

Is he a child of hell?
O clearly those soft brown eyes
speak volumes
of deviltry.
O surely those small pink teats
could suckle witches.
O those floppy ears
hear only the devil's hissing.
O that small pink tongue
will lick & lick at your heart
until only Satan may
slip in.

A fuzzy white dog?
Name him *Catch.*
A little black kitten?
She is *Jamara.*
A tiny brown rabbit?
Call her *Pyewackett.*

Beware, beware—
the soft, the innocent,

the kingdom of cuddly ones—
All these
expose you to the jealous tongues
of neighbors' flames,
all these
are the devil's snares!

Familiar familiars—
there is hellfire lurking
in the softest fur,
brimstone in the pinkest tongue,
damnation everlasting
in a *purr*.

Her Broom, or the Ride of the Witch

My broom
with its tuft of roses
beckoning at the black,
with its crown of thistles,
prickling the sky,
with its carved crescents
winking silverly
at Diana,
with its thick brush
of peacock feathers
sweeping the night,
with its triangle
of glinting fur.

I ride
over the roofs
of doom.
I ride
while he thinks me safe
in our bed.
My forehead
he thinks that scraggly
other broom,
my hips that staff,
my sex that stump
of blackthorn
& of twine.

Ah, I will ride
over the skies—
orange as apricots
slashed red
with pomegranate clouds—
He will think me safe in our bed.
He will think I fear
such fabulous
flight.

It is his bed I fear!
I will burn the clouds
with my marvelous broom.
I will catch Persephone's seeds
on my flaming tongue.
Ah—if I burn for this,
how beautiful my ashes—
& how beautiful,
my beautiful, comet-tailed
broom!

Love Magick

Oh for a candle I could light
to draw you closer . . .
Oh for a poppet
made like you,
with your own lovely body
sewn again of cloth,
with your own pale
unseeing eyes,
with your own cock sweetly curving,
remade in wax or clay. . . .

Oh for an herb
to place upon my tongue
to bring your tongue
to mine. . . .

Oh for a potion
I could drink
or slip to you
at some stale
dinner party. . . .

Oh for your nail parings . . .
Oh for your hairs . . .
stirred in a brew,
baked in a millet cake. . . .

I would make a stew,
a soup, a witch's mix
to bring your lovely thighs
on mine.

I would boil bats if not babies
& toads if not theologians
to make you care. . . .

I would enter your blood
like malaria, enter your eyes
like laser beams, enter your palms
like the holy spirit
causing stigmata
to a sex-starved saint!

Oh love,
I would spell you
evol
if mere anagrams
would bring you
near. . . .

But I spell you *love*
& still
you do not
hear.

Bitter Herb

If you would poison your mind
with the bitter herb of self-hate,
nothing can save you:
not the lover who comes in the night
smelling of pitch & brimstone,
not the husband who comes in the light
smelling of hay & the golden turds of mares,
not the mother with her poisoned apple,
not the daughter with her wreaths of roses & opium poppies,
not the sister with her rosemary & rue,
not the brother with the mandrake root.

Having driven out the demons of the past
we find them now within.
No witches burn in the market
but our minds revolve upon their own spits;
no crucifixion upon Calvary
but a daily torture in the hills of the skull,
no smell of burning female flesh upon the heath,
but the acrid odor of the heart slowly smoldering.

What witchcraft will it take
to bend this world to our will?
Must we burn poisonous herbs
to kill the poisons in the streams?
Must we wear poultices of Henbane
& Deadly Nightshade
against the very air?

O take this garlic rosary,
this token of death's breath,
this possessed vegetable,
this bulb of dried desire.
I am sick of haunting myself
from within
like an old house.
I would be happier
as a hunted witch.

For All Those Who Died

For all those who died—
stripped naked, shaved, shorn.

For all those who screamed
in vain to the Great Goddess
only to have their tongues
ripped out at the root.

For all those who were pricked, racked, broken on the wheel
for the sins of their Inquisitors.

For all those whose beauty
stirred their torturers to fury;
& for all those whose ugliness did the same.

For all those who were neither ugly nor beautiful,
but only women who would not submit.

For all those quick fingers
broken in the vise.

For all those soft arms
pulled from their sockets.

For all those budding breasts
ripped with hot pincers.

For all those midwives killed merely for the sin
of delivering man
to an imperfect world.

For all those witch-women, my sisters,
who breathed freer
as the flames took them,

knowing as they shed
their female bodies,
the seared flesh falling like fruit
in the flames,

that death alone would cleanse them
of the sin for which they died

the sin of being born a woman,
who is more than the sum
of her parts.

A DEADLY HERBAL IN VERSE

Mandrake

O *Mandragora*
herbal puppet,
little man dancing
with your great tap root,
small song-&-dance man
cloven-hoofed as the Devil—
no wonder you make such noise!

O Mandrake
putting out fine root hairs . . .
for centuries
Pythagoras & Theophrastus
sang your praises—
blessed you as aphrodisiac
& soporific,
blasted your resemblance
to man.

Like man you are tricky, devious,
double-natured.
Like man you curse & bless.
Like man you are a poisoner
& a love-bringer.
Like man you take
what you can.

O Mandrake,
bringer of fruitfulness & potency,
lamp in the darkness,
killer of starving dogs,
shrieker, gallowsman, dragon-doll—
in Biblical times,
you were thought beneficent
but gradually the Devil won.

You grew at the foot
of the gallows,
lapping up dead men's sperm,
giving birth only
to death.

& yet we all give birth to death,
& your other attributes—
O bringer of treasure, sensuality, love,
success in battle—
also lead to death.

So dance, little Mandrake,
in your doubleness.
Rejoice at the gallows' foot.
You are indeed a dress rehearsal for man,
& we shall join you
soon enough
underground.

Henbane

Herba Apollinaris,
Circe's herb,
the Delphic Priestesses'
wine—
is it you
with your jagged leaves
& sickly flowers
who turn men
to swine?
Is it you
who pluck the prophecies
from smoke,
above the great Omphalos
in the gorge?

Common as the lowly potato,
but with the power
to bring oblivion or death,
Ulysses lost
his sailors
to your spell,
while that mild witch, Circe,
wove harmonies
upon her magic loom
where the fabric
flickered
like firelight.

Sleepy beasts
beneath her shuttlecock,
the wolves & lions loll
like aging dogs . . .
the witch tickles
their bellies.

Half girl, half goddess,
all enchantress,
Circe dreams of Odysseus,
luring him
with bright thoughts,
bright threads,
& honeyed wine.

Was it you, Henbane,
turning beastly men
to loving beasts?
Is that why Circe
loved you so?

Until Ulysses
stormed in
with his broadsword,
the master mariner,
the son of gods
of old,
& used to taming women
to his will.

He took the witch
to bed—
not out of lust
for Hermes himself had ordered it—
(& Odysseus always
had a god at hand).

Was it Henbane
they smoked
before they went to bed?
Was it Henbane
that let their loving slip
from one slim night
into a whole fat year?

She sent him home
the long way
from her famous
bed of love,
through Death's cold vastnesses,
& pale Persephone's glacial halls.
Was it you
Henbane
who made the journey slow—

or was it Circe,
half girl, half goddess,
harmonizing on her lovely loom
while men lolled at her feet
like sleepy beasts . . .

O Circe,
you knew
a thing or two!

Thorn Apple

Datura stramonium
of the poisonous flowers—
even your smallest buds
are said to cause
madness, sleep & death,
but your spiny "apples,"
prickly & stiff as porcupines,
are the real villains,
& were much beloved
by Kali's worshipers,
the Thugs.

(O kill, kill, kill
but kill
in a goddess's name!)

Deadly poison
for arrow tips
& sacrificial victims' hearts—
you were also used
in love philters!

The cynic laughs,
knowing that love
is the first poison—
the poison
that takes the soul,
the mind,

& all the organs
down below.

(O kill, kill, kill
but kill
in a goddess's name!)

Venus, Kali, the Great Mother,
the God of the Witches—
what does it matter?
Love potion or poison,
it is the same drink
that brings oblivion
in the end.

Love-will, Sorcerer's herb,
Jimson weed,
you were used by brothel keepers
to seduce the innocent,
& witches brewed you
for their flying ointments.
The soldiers of Jamestown
made merry with your juice.

It was a new country
but the herbs were old.

The poisons link us
to antiquity—
the poisons & the love philters.
Down through the Ages
we are joined by vines;
we wear garlands
of poisonous berries
like jewels.

Green as innocence,
green as love of death,
we bud, we flower, we fall—

& ancient herbs
grow
out of our blind
eyes.

Deadly Nightshade

When the Deadly Nightshade flowers,
dreamy-eyed girls
open their lids
for their lovers.
Maenads fall upon men
dripping with dreams.
& children die
from the sweetest
of inky fruits.

Belladonna,
wine of the bacchanals,
you are indeed the witch's berry,
I look into your open eye & see
Dionysian orgies,
women in love with death,
dying with the widest
& brightest of eyes.

Have you no shame at all
Atropa belladonna?
The other herbs pretend to be angelic,
but you freely play
the Devil's part.

Dwaleberry, Sorcerer's cherry,
Murderer's berry——
your sweetness bursts

on the tongue,
the lungs relax,
& death comes
merely
from refusing
air.

Monkshood

Most beautiful of poisons,
border-plant,
wearing your small green cowl,
little friar, little murderer,
aconitine flows
from your roots
to your deep purple flowers,
small deceiver,
centerpiece
for a poisonous
feast.

A few leaves
in the salad,
a few seeds
in the soup,
a thick root
to flavor
the stock—
& it is all over.

Let the lover beware
who buys you
for love philters.
The dose is deceptive.
One pinch leads to passion
but two will surely lead
to death.

Yet you twinkle
little blue bell
at the edge
of the garden,
wearing no warning
about your slim green neck.

Wolfsbane, Friar's cap,
Chariot of Venus—

how many may claim
to be poisonous
head to toe?

That honor—
Friar Death—
belongs to you.

VIII

❖

At the Edge of the Body
(1979)

At the Edge of the Body

At the edge of the body
there is said to be
a flaming halo—
yellow, red, blue
or pure white,
taking its color
from the state
of the soul.

Cynics scoff.
Scientists make graphs
to refute it.
Editorial writers,
journalists, & even
certain poets,
claim it is only mirage,
trumped-up finery,
illusory feathers,
spiritual shenanigans,
humbug.

But in dreams
we see it,
& sometimes even waking.
If the spirit is a bride
about to be married to God,
this is her veil.

Do *I* believe it?
Do I squint
& regard the perimeter
of my lover's body,
searching for some sign
that his soul
is about to ignite
the sky?

Without squinting,
I *almost* see it.
An angry red aura
changing to white,
the color of peace.

I gaze at the place
where he turns into air
& the flames of his skin
combine
with the flames of the sky,
proving
the existence
of both.

Self-Portrait in Shoulder Stand

Old bag of bones
upside down,
what are you searching for
in poetry,
in meditation?

The mother you never had?

The child in you
that you did not conceive?

Death?

Ease from the fear of death?

Revelation?

Dwelling in the house of clouds
where you imagine
you once lived?

"Born alone,
we depart alone."
Someone said that
during meditation
& I nearly wept.

Oh melancholy lady
behind your clown face,
behind your wisecracks—
how heady it is
to let the ideas rush to your brain!

But even upside down,
you are sad.

Even upside down,
you think of your death.
Even upside down,
you curse the emptiness.

Meditating
on the immobile lotus,
your mind takes flight
like a butterfly
& dabbles in bloodred poppies
& purple heather.

Defying gravity,
defying death,
what makes you think
the body's riddle
is better solved
upside down?

Blood rushes to your head
like images that come too fast
to write.
After a life held in the double grips
of gravity & time,
after a headfirst birth
out of your mother's bowels
& into the earth,
you practice for the next.

You make your body light
so that in time,
feetfirst,
you will be born
into the sky.

My Death

"Death is our eternal companion," Don
Juan said with a most serious air. *"It is
always to our left, at an arm's length. . . .
It has always been watching you. It always
will until the day it taps you."*

                    —Carlos Castaneda

My death
looks exactly like me.
She lives to my left,
at exactly an arm's length.
She has my face, hair, hands;
she ages
as I grow older.

Sometimes, at night,
my death awakens me
or else appears in dreams
I did not write.
Sometimes a sudden wind
blows from nowhere,
& I look left
& see my death.

Alive, I write
with my right hand only.
When I am dead,
I shall write with my left.

But later I will have to write
through others.
I may appear
to future poets
as their deaths.

Zen & the Art of Poetry

Letting the mind go,
letting the pen, the breath,
the movement of images in & out
of the mouth
go calm, go rhythmic
as the rise & fall of waves,
as one sits in the lotus position
over the world,
holding the pen so lightly
that it scarcely stains the page,
holding the breath
in the glowing cage of the ribs,
until the heart
is only a living lantern
fueled by breath,
& the pen writes
what the heart wills
& the whole world goes out,
goes black,
but for the hard, clear stars
below.

The Xylophone of the Spine

The cosmos has played
on the xylophone
of my spine,
hitting each vertebra
with a single clear-pitched tone,
making my backbone
reverberate
with the fleshly echo
of the music
of the spheres.

When the flesh falls from these bones,
the notes will be clearer.
When the skin withers
& the spirit sails out
clear as the autumn air,
crisp as the falling leaves,
shining as the waters of our planet
seen from afar
by creatures who are made
of melody,
& who are invisible,
untouchable & far
except when they come to earth
to make music
on our fragile bones.

Aura

I sit in the black leather chair
meditating
on the plume of smoke that rises
in the air,
riffling the pages of my life
as if it were a book of poems,
flipping through
past & future.

If I go back, back, back,
riding the plume of smoke,
I find I died
in childbirth in another life,
died by fire in the life before that,
died by water twice, or more.

I pick out days
& relive them
as if I were trying on dresses.

When the future beckons,
I follow,
riding another plume of smoke,
feeling the barrier
between skin & air
evaporate,
& my body disappear
like the myth it is.

My cheeks burn against the air,
flaming where two elements collide
& intermingle
becoming one.

Oh explosion at the body's edge!
I live on a ledge of time,
gazing
at the infinite.

The Keys

Broken ivories
playing
the blue piano
of the sea.

We have come
from the bitter city
to heal ourselves.
We have come
looking for a patch of beach
not yet built into a fortress
of real-estate greed,
a coral reef
not yet picked clean
of buried treasure,
not yet bare of birds.

The first night in the Keys,
I dreamed I was a bird
soaring over a hilly city,
soaring & dipping
like a gull or egret.
& I thought:
"Ah—this is a flying dream!
Enjoy it."

But I really think
that my soul

had been transported
for a night
into the body of
a bird
& I was *flying*.

I woke up
exhausted,
arms weary,
eyes red.
The beach was dazzling
with its white sand,
the sun blinding,
& I seemed to know the palm trees
from above
as well as below.

They root in the sand
with elephant feet,
yet they also root
their delicate fronds
in air.
& these are a comfort
as you fly
half bird, half human
through a dream of sky.

Everything was new
to a spirit
so divided
between two kingdoms.
The water was alive
with fish,
the air with birds
& palm fronds,
clouds, thunderous presences
of rain
gathering & parting,
& fiery sun playing through.

I knew
that I stood
on a patch of earth
connected to the sky,
that my heart beat
with the sea,
that my arms moved
with the clouds,
that my flesh
was finally irrelevant
though it surrounded me
as the case of a piano
surrounds its strings,
while the fingers play
on the ivory keys
& the human music
rises to the sky.

The Poetry Suit

I put on` my poetry suit.
The prose falls away
like a dream I cannot remember,
the images unraveling like threads
in a cheap dress, sewn in Hong Kong
to feed the hungry mouths
of sweet-faced Chinese children.

Now I am in my poetry suit.
I zip myself into it,
pink as flesh, tight as the suit
I was born in, & looking
seamless as a perfect poem,
gleaming as the golden fleece,
slim as a stripper at the Crazy Horse Saloon,
transparent as silk stockings,
& smelling of jasmine & tea rose.

But what was that old perfume
I left in the pocket,
that cotton ball soaked
in Bal à Versailles,
that yellowing glacé glove
that lacks a mate,
that fine cambric handkerchief
brown with dried blood
from an old nosebleed?

Even poetry, pure as nothing
but snow or music,
drags life along
in its hidden pockets.

Oh for an art
that is not made of words
with all their odors
& indiscretions.

The Buddha in the Womb

Bobbing in the waters of the womb,
little godhead, ten toes, ten fingers
& infinite hope,
sails upside down through the world.

My bones, I know, are only a cage
for death.
Meditating, I can see my skull,
a death's head,
lit from within
by candles
which are possibly the suns
of other galaxies.

I know that death
is a movement toward light,
a happy dream
from which you are loath to awaken,
a lover left
in a country
to which you have no visa,
& I know that the horses of the spirit
are galloping, galloping, galloping
out of time
& into the moment called NOW.

Why then do I care
for this upside-down Buddha

bobbling through the world,
his toes, his fingers
alive with blood
that will only sing & die.

There is a light in my skull
& a light in his.
We meditate on our bones only
to let them blow away
with fewer regrets.

Flesh is merely a lesson.
We learn it
& pass on.

Without Parachutes

*The experiencer of fear is not an observer of
it; he is fear itself, the very instrument of
fear.*

—J. Krishnamurti

In dreams I descend
into the cave of my past:
a child with a morgue-tag
on its toe,
the terrible metal squeaking
of the morgue-drawers,
& the chilly basement
& the slam of doors.

Or else I am setting up dreamhouse,
with the wife
of my second ex-husband.
She complains of him
with breaking sorrow—
& I comfort her.
(She only married him, it seems, for me.)

Sometimes I wake up naked
in Beverly Hills—
the table set for ten, a formal dinner—
a studio chief on my left side,
a fabled actor on my right.

Across the table,
Greta Garbo, Scott Fitzgerald,
John F. Kennedy & Marilyn Monroe—

& I alone not properly dressed for dinner,
& besides unprepared
for the final exam,
in which our immortality
will be tested,
& one of us shall perish
as dessert.

Send parachutes & kisses!
Send them quick!
I am descending into the cave
of my own fear.
My feet are weighted
with the leg-irons of the past.
The elevator plummets
in the shaft.

Trapped, trapped in the bowels
of my dream,
locked in the cellar
by myself the jailer.
Rats and spiders scuttle
through the coal bin.
I cower in the corner.

I am fear.

If God Is a Dog

If God is a dog drowsing,
contemplating
the quintessential dogginess
of the universe, of the whole
canine race, why are we
uneasy?

No dog I know
would hurl thunderbolts,
or plant plague germs,
or shower us with darts
of pox or gonococci.
No. He lies on his back
awaiting
the cosmic belly rub.
He wags his tail signifying
universal love.
He frolics and cavorts
because he has just
taken a galactic shit
& found it good.
All dogs are blessed;
they live in the now.

But God is all too human.
Somehow we have spelled his name
wrong, got it backward,
aroused his growl.

God drowses
like a lazy old man
bored
with our false
alarms.

Best Friends

We made them
in the image of our fears
to cry at doors,
at partings—even brief,
to beg for food at table,
& to look at us with those big
aching eyes,
& stay beside us
when our children flee,
& sleep upon our beds
on darkest nights,
& cringe at thunder
as in our own
childhood
frights.

We made them sad-eyed,
loving, loyal, scared
of life without us.
We nurtured their dependency
& grief.
We keep them as reminders of our fear.
We love them
as the unacknowledged hosts
of our own terror
of the grave—abandonment.

Hold my paw
for I am dying.

Sleep upon my coffin;
wait for me,
sad-eyed
in the middle of the drive
that curves beyond the cemetery wall.

I hear your bark,
I hear your mournful howl—
oh may all dogs that I have ever loved
carry my coffin,
howl at the moonless sky,
& lie down with me sleeping
when I die.

The Exam Dream

In a season of deaths,
when the dead ones, the great ones
were falling all around,
when the leaves were turning
scarlet, crimson, brown as blood,
when the birches trembled
& the oaks turned gold,

I dreamed,
perhaps for the last time,
the old exam-dream:
a history course
& I had not read a word.
Though I took my degree Phi Bete
with every honor,
I trembled in my dream
that I would fail.

Oh the terror
in the college corridor!
The fear of reprisals,
the fear of death.
The history of the world
is blank to me.
The only thing I know
is certain
death.

How are we tested?
Why do our minds
go blank?
Why the exam room,
courtroom,
why the witness stand?
Even the Phi Bete kids
must fail in dreams;
A's & F's are equalized
by sleep.

Perhaps we are tested by mortality.
No childhood of anxiety
& pain,
no eyes behind glasses
searching flyspeck print
can spare us
from the certain truth
we fail.

Teach us to live
each day
as if our last.

Teach us the present tense,
teach us the word.
Teach us to take air in
& let it out
without the fearful catch
of breath on death.

Truce with the cosmos,
soul at peace within,
we may stop dreaming
that we fail
life's school.

Our lives are in your hands,
our deaths assured.
Between this knowledge
& our schooldays
fall our dreams.

His Tuning of the Night

All night he lies awake tuning the sky,
tuning the night with its fat crackle of static,
with its melancholy love songs crooning
across the rainy air above Verdun
& the autobahn's blue suicidal dawn.

Wherever he lives there is the same unwomaned bed,
the ashtrays overflowing their reproaches,
his stained fingers on the tuning bar, fishing
for her voice in a deep mirrorless pond,
for the tinsel & elusive fish
(brighter than pennies in water & more wished upon)—
the copper-colored daughter of the pond god.

He casts for her, the tuning bar his rod,
but only long-dead lovers with their griefs
haunt him in Piaf's voice—
(as if a voice could somehow only die
when it was sung out, utterly).

He finally lies down and drowns the light
but the taste of her rises, brackish,
from the long dark water of her illness
& his grief is terrible as drowning
when he reaches for the radio again.

In the daytime, you hardly know him;
he walks in a borrowed calm.

You cannot sense
his desperation in the dawn
when the abracadabras of the birds
conjure another phantom day.

He favors cities which blaze all night,
hazy mushrooms of light under the blue
& blinking eyes of jets.
But when the lamps across the way go under,
& the floorboards settle,
& the pipes fret like old men gargling——
he is alone with his mouthful of ghosts,
his tongue bitter with her unmourned death,
& the terrible drowning.

I watch from my blue window
knowing he does not trust me,
though I know him as I know my ghosts,
though I know his drowning,
though, since that night when all harmony broke for me,
I have been trying to tune the sky.

The Deaths of the Goddesses

It used to be hard
for women,
snowed in their white lives,
white lies,
to write books
with that fine frenzy
which commends genius
to posterity,
yet estranges it
from its closest
friends.

Women were friends to all,
& being too friendly
they could not command
the unfriendly prerogatives
of genius,
though some were
geniuses still,
destroying
only themselves
with the torment
of the unfriendly ghost
trapped in a friendly
form.

Oh the women who died
dissembling friendship

for the world!
Oh the women who turned
the dagger inward
when it wished
to go out,
who impaled themselves
on Womanhood itself!

No vampire
could be
as greedy for blood,
no father or husband
as bullying.
A woman punishing herself
with her own pain
is a fierce opponent indeed.

It is self against self,
dagger to dagger,
blood of her blood,
blood of her daughter,
blood of her mother,
her menses, her moon,
all pooled together,
one crimson sea.

It is the awful *auto da fé,*
the sublime *seppuku,*
Santa Sebastiana
as archer
& victim too.

The arrow flies from her bow.
She runs, fleet as Diana,
& stops it
with her breast.

303

Enough!
cried the Women-Who-Cared.
Henceforth we will turn
our anger where it belongs.
We will banish the whitest lies.
We will speak the black truth as it is.
Our fathers—we spit back their sperm.
Our husbands—we spit back their names.
Our brothers—we suck back our love.

The self-righteous inherit the earth,
& anger speaks louder than love.
Love is a softness
the weak cannot afford,
& sex a Darwinian bribe.

But who wants the earth as a gift
when it is empty as space,
when women grow hard
as bronze madonnas
& Diana loves only her stag?

When Persephone stays in hell
the entire year,
then how can spring
begin?

The Truce Between the Sexes

For a long time unhappy
with my man,
I blamed men,
blamed marriage, blamed
the whole bleeding world,
Because I could not lie in bed with him
without lying to him
or else to myself,
& lying to myself
became increasingly hard
as my poems
struck rock.

My life & my poems lived apart;
I had to marry them,
& marrying them
meant divorcing him,
divorcing the lie.

Now I lie in bed
with my poems on the sheets
& a man I love
sleeping or reading
at my side.

Because I love him,
I do not think of him
as "Men,"

but as my friend.
Hate generalizes;
love is particular.

He is not Men, man, male—
all those maddening m's
muttering like machine-gun spittle,
but only a person like me,
dreaming, vulnerable, scared,
his dreams
opening into rooms
where the chairs
are wishes you can sit on
& the rugs are wonderful
with oriental birds.

The first month we lived together
I was mad with joy,
thinking that a person with a penis
could dream, tell jokes, even cry.
Now I find it usual,
& when other women sputter
of their rage,
I look at them blankly,
half comprehending
those poor medieval creatures
from a dark, dark age.

I wonder about myself.
Was I always so fickle?
Must politics always be personal?
If I struck oil,
would I crusade
for depletion allowances?

Erica, Erica,
you are hard on yourself.
Lie back & enjoy the cease-fire.

Trouble will come again.
Sex will grow horns & warts.
The white sheets of this bed
will be splattered with blood.
Just wait.

But I don't believe it.
There will be trouble enough,
but a different sort.

Depression in Early Spring

Meathooks, notebooks,
the whole city sky palely flaming
& spectral bombs
hitting that patch of river
I see from my eastern window.

The poets are dead, the city dying.
Anne, Sylvia, Keats
with his passionate lungs,
Berryman jumping from the bridge & waving,
all the dreamers dead
of their own dreams.

Why have I stayed on as Horatio?
Anne sends poems from the grave,
Sylvia, letters.
John Keats's ghostly cough
comes through the wall board.
What am I doing here?
Why contend?

I am a corpse who moves a pen that writes.
I am a vessel for a voice that echoes.
I write a novel & annihilate whole forests.
I rearrange the cosmos by an inch.

Blood & Honey

I began by loving women
& the love turned
to bitterness.

My mother, the bitter,
whose bitter lesson—
trust no one,
especially no one male—
caused me to be naive
for too many years,
in mere rebellion
against that bitterness.

If she was Medea,
I would be Candide
& bleed in every sexual war,
& water my garden with menstrual blood
& grow the juiciest fruits.

(Like the woman
who watered her roses with blood
& won all the prizes,
though no one knew why.)

If she was Lady Macbeth,
I would be Don Quixote—
& never pass up a windmill
without a fight,

& never choose discretion
over valor.

My valor was often foolish.
I was rash
(though others called me brave).
My poems were red flags
To lure the bulls.
The picadors smelled blood
& jabbed my novels.

I had only begun
by loving women—
& ended by hating their deceit,
hating the hate
they feed their daughters,
hating the self-hate
they feed themselves,
hating the contempt
they feed their men,
as they claim weakness—
their secret strength.

For who can be crueler
than a woman
who is cruel
out of her impotence?
& who can be meaner
than a woman
who desires
the only room with a view?

Even in chess
she shouts:
"Off with their heads!"
& the poor king
walks one step forward,
one step back.

But I began
by loving women,
loving myself
despite my mother's lesson,
loving my ten fingers,
ten toes, my puckered navel,
my lips that are too thick
& my eyes the color of ink.

Because I believed in them,
I found gentle men.
Because I loved myself,
I was loved.
Because I had faith,
the unicorn licked my arm,
the rabbit nestled in my skirts,
the griffin slept
curled up at the bottom
of my bed.

Bitter women,
there is milk under this poem.
What you sow in blood
shall be harvested in honey.

Woman Enough

Because my grandmother's hours
were apple cakes baking,
& dust motes gathering,
& linens yellowing
& seams and hems
inevitably unraveling—
I almost never keep house—
though really I *like* houses
& wish I had a clean one.

Because my mother's minutes
were sucked into the roar
of the vacuum cleaner,
because she waltzed with the washer-dryer
& tore her hair waiting for repairmen—
I send out my laundry,
& live in a dusty house,
though really I *like* clean houses
as well as anyone.

I am woman enough
to love the kneading of bread
as much as the feel
of typewriter keys
under my fingers—
springy, springy.
& the smell of clean laundry
& simmering soup

are almost as dear to me
as the smell of paper and ink.

I wish there were not a choice;
I wish I could be two women.
I wish the days could be longer.
But they are short.
So I write while
the dust piles up.

I sit at my typewriter
remembering my grandmother
& all my mothers,
& the minutes they lost
loving houses better than themselves—
& the man I love cleans up the kitchen
grumbling only a little
because he knows
that after all these centuries
it is easier for him
than for me.

Assuming Our Dominance

Assuming our dominance
over the creatures of earth—
dog, cat, sparrow,
tiny field mouse
(who lives in our kitchen
as a blur of light
running past the edges
of our sight)—
how can we understand humility?

The mouse-droppings
in the silverware drawer
annoy us.
The infinite insects
creep out of the walls
one by one,
only to be slammed
under our soles.
Our souls are heavy
with the deaths of animals.
Ocelot, beaver, fox
& even the ugly
slant-eyed mink
give their skins
to women
who are no more beautiful to God
than they.
The lowly roach,

or the tick
that seeks admission to our bed
on the back of a gentle dog,
is beloved by some creator.

Assuming our dominance
has made us mad,
has made the fragrant earth
into a place
where the mice that fill the edges
of our eyes
& scuttle past our countertops
& dreams—
are fears, the lurking fears
of our own kind.

House-Hunting in the Bicentennial Year

Looking for a home, America,
we have split & crisscrossed
you from your purple seashores
to your nongrip, nonslip
motel bathrooms,
from the casinos at Reno
to the crystalline shores of Lake Tahoe,
from the giant duck in Southampton
(which is really an egg shop)
to the giant hotdog in L.A.
(which is really a hotdog stand)
to the giant artichoke in Castroville, CA,
the heart of the artichoke
country,
& still we are homeless
this 1976.

America,
we have met your brokers.
They are fiftyish ladies in hairnets,
or fiftyish ladies in blue & silver hair like mink coats
or flirty fiftyish ladies
getting blonder every winter.
They tout your federal brickwork
& your random hand-pegged floorboards.
Like witches, they advertise your gingerbread houses,
your "high ranches," your split-levels,

your Victorians, your widows' walks,
your whaling towns,
instead of wailing walls,
your Yankee New England spunk,
your hospitality, your tax rates,
your school systems,
with or without busing,
your friendly dogs
& philosophical cats.

America,
we have ridden through your canyons,
passes, dried-up rivers,
past your flooded quarries, through your eroded arroyos.
We have sighted UFOs on the beach
at Malibu
& swum from pool to pool
like any Cheever hero
& lusted in motels like any Updike Christian.

America,
the open road is closing,
a tollbooth blocks the vista,
& even the toilets are pumped
with dimes as well as shit.
The fried clams on Cape Cod
are pressed from clam scraps.
The California carrot cake is rumored
to be made of soy.

The dreaming towers of Gotham
are sunk in garbage,
the bedrock softens,
the buildings list like drunks,
the Thanksgiving balloons are all deflated,
the Christmas trees don't even pretend to be green.

But we love you, America,
& we'll keep on hunting.
The dream house that we seek is just next door.
Switzerland is a heaven of chocolates
& tax breaks.
Barbados is sweet & black & tax-free.
Antigua is Britain by the sea.

But we're sticking around, America,
for the next earthquake,
kissing the ground
for the next Fourth of July.
We love you, America,
& we'll keep hunting.

There's a dream house waiting for us somewhere
with blooming cherry trees
& a FOR SALE sign,
with picture windows facing the Pacific
& dormer windows facing the Atlantic,
with coconut palms & flaming maples,
with shifting sand dunes
& canyons blazing with mustard,
with rabbits & rattlesnakes & nonpoisonous scorpions,
with raccoons who rattle the garbage
& meekly feeding deer who lap at salt licks
& pheasants who hop across the lawn in two-steps,
with loving dogs & aloof, contemplative cats,
with heated swimming pool & sauna
& an earthquake-proof Jacuzzi,
with carpeted carport & bathrooms
& plumbing so good it hums,
with neighbors who lend you organic sugar
& mailmen who are often women,
with huge supermarkets selling wine & kneesocks,
mangoes, papayas, & dogfood in fifty flavors,
with nearby movie theaters playing Bergman & Fellini
without dubbing,

with resident symphony orchestras
down the block,
but no rock stars living right next door.

We know we'll find you someday
if not in this life, America,
then in the next,
if not in this solar system,
then in another.
We're ready to move, America.
We've called our unscrupulous movers
who always break everything & demand to be paid in cash,
& we have our downpayment in hand.
We lust for a big fat mortgage.
We've pulled up our city roots
& we've packed our books, our banjo & our dog
in a bright red gypsy wagon
with low gas mileage.

All we need is the house,
all we need is the listing.
We're ready to move, America,
but we don't know
where.

January in New York

Black ship of night
sailing through the world
& the moon an orange slice
tangy to the teeth
of lovers who lie
under it,
sucking it.

Somewhere there are palm trees;
somewhere the sea
bluely gathers itself up
& lets itself fall again
into green;
somewhere the spangles
of light on the ocean
dazzle the eyes;
but here in the midnight city,
the black ship of night
has docked
for a long, dark stay,
& even the citrus moon
with its pockets of juice
cannot sweeten the dark.

Then the snow begins,
whirling over the Pole,
gathering force over Canada,
sprinkling the Great Lakes with sugar
which drowns in their deep black cups;
it is drawn to the spires of New York
& the flurries come
scampering at first,
lighthearted, crystalline, white,
but finally
sucked into the city
as into a black hole
in space.

The sky is suddenly pink—
pink as flesh: breasts,
babies' bottoms. Night is
day; day is whiter than the desert;
the city stops like a heart;
pigeons dip & veer
& come to rest
under the snow-hatted
watertanks.

New England Winter

Testing the soul's mettle,
the frost heaves
holes in the roads
to the heart,
the glass forest
raises up its branches
to praise all things
that catch the light
then melt.
The forest floor is white,
but here & there a boulder rises
with its glacial arrogance
& brooks that bubble
under sheets of ice
remind us that the tundra of the soul
will soften
just a little
towards the spring.

Jubilate Canis

(With apologies to Christopher Smart)

For I will consider my dog Poochkin
(& his long-lost brothers, Chekarf & Dogstoyevsky).
For he is the reincarnation of a great canine poet.
For he barks in meter, & when I leave him alone
his yelps at the door are epic.
For he is white, furry & resembles a bathmat.
For he sleeps at my feet as I write
& therefore is my greatest critic.
For he follows me into the bathroom
& faithfully pees on paper.
For he is *almost* housebroken.
For he eats the dogfood I give him
but also loves Jarlsberg and Swiss cheese.
For he disdains nothing that reeks—
whether feet or roses.
For to him, all smells are created equal by God—
both turds and perfumes.
For he loves toilet bowls no less than soup bowls.
For by watching him, I have understood democracy.
For by stroking him, I have understood joy.
For he turns his belly toward God
& raises his paws & penis in supplication.
For he hangs his pink tongue out of his mouth
like a festival banner for God.
For though he is male, he has pink nipples on his belly

323

like the female.
For though he is canine, he is more humane
than most humans.
For when he dreams he mutters in his sleep
like any poet.
For when he wakes he yawns & stretches
& stands on his hind legs to greet me.
For, after he shits, he romps and frolics
with supreme abandon.
For, after he eats, he is more contented
than any human.
For in every room he will find the coolest corner,
& having found it, he has the sense to stay there.
For when I show him my poems,
he eats them.
For an old shoe makes him happier than a Rolls-Royce
makes a rock star.
For he has convinced me of the infinite wisdom
of dog-consciousness.
For, thanks to Poochkin, I praise the Lord
& no longer fear death.
For when my spirit flees my body through my nostrils,
may it sail into the pregnant belly
of a furry bitch,
& may I praise God always
as a dog.

I Live in New York

I am happiest
near the ocean,
where the changing light
reminds me of my death
& the fact that it need not be fatal—

yet I perch here
in the midst of the city
where the traffic dulls my senses,
where my ears scream at sirens,
where transistor radio blasts
invade my poems
like alien war chants.

But I never walk
the streets of New York
without hoping for the end
of the world.

How many years
before the streets return to flowers?
How many centuries
before the towers fall?

In my mind's eye,
New York falls to ruins.
Butterflies alight upon the stones
and poppies spring
out of the asphalt fields.

Why do I stay here
when I love the ocean?
Because the ocean lulls me
with its peace.
Eternity is coming soon enough.
As monks sleep
in their own coffins,

I live in New York.

Flight to Catalina

On a darkening planet
speeding
toward our death,
we pierce a rosy cloud
& hit clean air,
we glide above
the red infernal smog,
we leave the mammon city
far behind.

Here——where the air is clear
as nothing,
where cactus pads
are prickly as stars,
where buffalo chips
are gilded by the sun
& the moon tastes like a peppermint——
we land.

"Have we flown to heaven?"
I inquired
(& meant it).
The airport was a leveled
mountaintop.
We took the cloudbank
at a tilt
& bumped the runway
just ten degrees from crashing,
certain death.

If I'm to die, God,
let me die flying!
Fear is worse than death—
I know that now.
The cloudbanks of my life
have silver linings.
Beyond them:
cactus pads,
clear earth,
dear sky.

Good Carpenters

I mourn a dead friend, like myself, a good carpenter.

——Pablo Neruda about César Vallejo

I looked at the book.
"It will stand," I thought.
Not a palace
built by a newspaper czar,
nor a mud hovel
that the sea will soften,
but a good house of words
near the sea
with everything plumb.
That is the most I can ask.

I have cut the wood myself
from my own forests,
I have sanded it smooth
with the grain.
I have left knotholes
for the muse to whistle through
——old siren that she is.

At least the roof does not leak.
& the fireplace is small
but it draws.
The wind whips the house

but it stands.
& the waves lick
the pilings
with their tongues
but at least they do not suck me
out to sea.
The sea is wordless
but it tries to talk to us.
We carpenters are also translators.
We build with sounds, with whispers & with wind.
We try to speak the language of the sea.

We want to build to last
yet change forever.
We want to be as endless as the sea.
& yet she mocks us
with her barnacles & rust stains;
she tells us what we build will also fall.

Our words are grains of sand,
our walls are wood,
our windowpanes are sprayed with solemn salt.
We whisper, as we build, "Forever please,"
—by which we mean at least for thirty years.

People Who Live

People who live by the sea
understand eternity.
They copy the curves of the waves,
their hearts beat with the tides,
& the saltiness of their blood
corresponds with the sea.

They know that the house of flesh
is only a sandcastle
built on the shore,
that skin breaks
under the waves
like sand under the soles
of the first walker on the beach
when the tide recedes.

Each of us walks there once,
watching the bubbles
rise up through the sand
like ascending souls,
tracing the line of the foam,
drawing our index fingers
along the horizon
pointing home.

Unrequited

Parachuting
down through clouds
shaped like whales & sharks,
dolphins & penguins,
pelicans & gulls,
we reach
the purple hills
of a green-hearted island
ringed
with volcanic rock
bathed
by cobalt waters
reefed
by whitest coral
tenanted
by sea urchins & sponge
& visited
by barracuda
& tourists.

The dictator
of this island
is the sun.
The Secret Police
is the sweet
fragrance of cane.
Frangipani grows
in the uplands;

the salt flats
reek
by the sea.

I want to buy it,
to hide here,
to stay,
to teach all the people
to write,
to orchestrate the stars
in the palm trees
& teach the jellyfish
not to bite.

Oh dark volcanic
wine!
Oh collapsed parachute
filled with kisses!
Oh blue-bottle bits
ground
into jewels
by the sand!

Whoever loves islands
must love the sea,
& the sea
loves no one
but herself.

Summoning the Muse to a New House

Woodsprites
& deer arrive;
raccoons hitch a night ride
in the still car
& eat all the Life Savers
from the glove compartment;
woodchucks feast
on the vegetable seedlings;
a swarm of honeybees
breaks loose from a neighboring hive
& storms my third-floor
study window
in search of honey;
a bitch in heat
seeks out
our horny dog;
a hawk nests
in the fir tree
outside my window;
spiders weave
& spin their webs
from book to book,
from typewriter to ceiling beam;
but still the muse—
recalcitrant & slow—
does not arrive.

Her skirts snag
on the Rocky Mountains,
her blue hair trails
into the Pacific.
"You move too often,"
she accuses;
"I just get acclimated,
then you move again!"

Bitter muse,
you ought to be portable
as a typewriter.
You ought to be
transient as a spy,
adaptable as a diplomat,
self-effacing as the perfect
valet—
but you are not.

After all,
you are our mother;
unless we listen & obey,
you let us starve.

Come—there is honey here,
or at least, bees.
The honey's
in the making
if you come.

IX

❖

Ordinary Miracles

(1983)

Ordinary Miracles

Spring, rainbows,
ordinary miracles
about which
nothing new can be said.

The stars on a clear night
of a New England winter;
the soft air of the islands
along the old
Spanish Main;
pirate gold shining
in the palm;
the odor of roses
to the lover's nose . . .

There is no more poetry
to be written
of these things.
The rainbow's sudden revelation—
behold!
the cliché is true!
What can one say
but that?

So too
with you, little heart,
little miracle,

but you are
no less miracle
for being ordinary.

The Birth of the Water Baby

Little egg,
little nub,
full complement of
fingers, toes,
little rose blooming
in a red universe,
which once wanted you less
than emptiness,
but now holds you
fast,
containing your rapid heart
beat under its
slower one
as the earth
contains the sea.

O avocado pit
almost ready to sprout,
tiny fruit tree
within sight
of the sea,
little swimming fish,
little land lover,
hold on!
hold on!

Here, under my heart
you'll keep
till it's time
for us to meet,
& we come apart
that we may come
together,
& you are born
remembering
the wavesound
of my blood,
the thunder of my heart,
& like your mother
always dreaming
of the sea.

Another Language

The whole world is flat
& I am round.
Even women avert their eyes,
& men, embarrassed
by the messy way
that life turns into life,
look away,
forgetting they themselves
were once this roundness
underneath the heart,
this helpless fish
swimming in eternity.

The sound of O,
not the sound of I
embarrasses the world.
My friends, who voluntarily have made
their bodies flat,
their writings flat as grief,
look at me in disbelief.
What is this large unseemly thing—
a pregnant poet?
an enormous walking O?
Oh take all letters of the alphabet but that!
We speak the Esperanto of the flat!

Condemned to sign
language & silence, pregnant poems
for men to snicker at,
for women to denounce,
I live alone.
My world is round
& bounded by the mountain of my fear;
while all the great geographers agree
the world is flat
& roundness cannot be.

Anti-Conception

Could I unthink you,
little heart,
what would I do?
Throw you out
with last night's garbage,
undo my own decisions,
my own flesh
& commit you to the void
again?

Fortunately,
it is not my problem.
You hold on, beating
like a little clock,
Swiss in your precision,
Japanese in your tenacity,
& already having
your own karma,

while I, with my half-
hearted maternal urges,
my uncertainty that any creature
ever really creates
another (unless it be
herself), know you
as God's poem
& myself merely as publisher,
as midwife,

as impresario,
oh, even, if you will,
as loathèd producer
of your *Grand Spectacle:*
you are the star,
& like your humblest fan,
I wonder
(gazing at your image
on the screen)
who you really are.

Perishable Women

Perishable women—
the colonial graveyards
are strewn with your bones,
the islands of the Caribbean
are rich with your deaths.
You perished
like the creatures of the reefs,
bringing forth your kind.

Perishable women—
dying at twenty, twenty-three,
"Beloved wife & Tender Mother,"
long lamented by your husband
(& his wives),
survivors who outlasted you,
then died
the way you died.

Only the men lived on
to perish in the wars,
to die of sharkbite
or of fever, bloody flux,
the smallpox, even leprosy
or gout
(one ate well
on these islands in the sun).

Everyone was perishable;
children died
like flies;
& women died
in giving birth to children
who would die.

God was blamed,
& Nature's mighty hand
which wrought her handiwork
imperfectly,
& broke a hundred vessels
in the sea
that one whole
cup might be.

Perishable women—
smashed like pots
upon the floor beneath the wheel,
crushed like shells upon the beach,
like husks of coconut,
like bits of bottle glass.

At my age I'd be dead.

You would not be.

Anti-Matter

I am not interested
in my body—
the part that stinks
& rots & brings forth
life,
the part that the ground
swallows,
death giving birth
to death—
all of life,
considered
from the body's
point of view,
is a downhill slide
& all our small
preservatives
& griefs
cannot reverse the trend.

All sensualists
turn puritan
at the end—
turning up lust's soil
& finding bones
beneath the rich volcanic
dirt.

Some sleep in shrouds
& some in coffins;
some swear off
procreation, others turn
vegetarian, or worse:
they live on air——
on sheer platonic meals
of pure ideas;
once gluttons of the flesh,
they now become
gourmets of the mind.

How to resist that
when the spacious earth
swallows her children
so insatiably,
when all our space-age gods
are grounded,
& only the moan of pleasure
or the rasp of pain
can ever satisfy
the body's appetite?

& yet my body,
in its dubious wisdom,
led to yours;
& you may
puzzle out
this mystery in your turn.
Choose mind, choose body,
choose to wed the two;
many have tried
but few have done the deed.

Through you, perhaps,
I may at last succeed.

Nursing You

On the first night
of the full moon,
the primeval sack of ocean
broke,
& I gave birth to you
little woman,
little carrot top,
little turned-up nose,
pushing you out of myself
as my mother
pushed
me out of herself,
as her mother did,
& her mother's mother before her,
all of us born
of woman.

I am the second daughter
of a second daughter
of a second daughter,
but you shall be the first.
You shall see the phrase
''second sex''
only in puzzlement,
wondering how anyone,
except a madman,
could call you ''second''
when you are so splendidly

first,
conferring even on your mother
firstness, vastness, fullness
as the moon at its fullest
lights up the sky.

Now the moon is full again
& you are four weeks old.
Little lion, lioness,
yowling for my breasts,
growling at the moon,
how I love your lustiness,
your red face demanding,
your hungry mouth howling,
your screams, your cries
which all spell life
in large letters
the color of blood.

You are born a woman
for the sheer glory of it,
little redhead, beautiful screamer.
You are no second sex,
but the first of the first;
& when the moon's phases
fill out the cycle
of your life,
you will crow
for the joy
of being a woman,
telling the pallid moon
to go drown herself
in the blue ocean,
& glorying, glorying, glorying
in the rosy wonder
of your sunshining wondrous
self.

On Reading a Vast Anthology

Love, death, sleeping
with somebody else's husband
or wife——this
is what poetry is
about——Eskimo, Aztec,
or even Italian
Rinascimento,
or even the highfalutin Greeks
or noble Roman-O's.

O the constant turmoil
of the human species——
beds, graves, Spring with its
familiar rosebuds, the wrong beds,
the wrong graves, wars
unremembered & boundaries gained
only to be lost & lost
again
& lost roses whose lost
petals
reminded poets to *carpe, carpe*
diem with whoever's wife
or husband happened to
be handiest!

O Turmoil & Confusion——
you are my Muses!
O longing for a world

without death, without beds
divided by walls between houses!
All the beds float out to sea!
All the dying lovers wave
to the other dying lovers!
One of them writes on his mistress's skin as he floats.

He is the poet.
Not for this
will his life be spared.

This Element

Looking for a place
where we might turn off
the inner dialogue,
the monologue
of futures & regrets,
of pasts not past enough
& futures that may never come
to pass,
we found this boat
bobbing in the blue,
this refuge amid reefs,
this white hull
within this azure sibilance of sea,
this central rocking
so like the rocking
before birth.

Venus was born of the waters,
borne over them
to teach us about love—
our only sail
on the seas of our lives
as death is
our only anchor.

If we return again & again
to the sea
both in our dreams

& for our love affairs
it is because
this element alone
understands our pasts
& futures
& futures
as she makes them

one.

On the Avenue

Male?
Female?
God doesn't care
about sex
& the long tree-shaded avenue
toward death.

God says
the worm is as beautiful
as the apple it eats
& the apple as lovely
as the thick trunk
of the tree,
& the trunk of the tree
no more beautiful
than the air
surrounding it.

God doesn't care
about the battle
between the sexes
with which we amuse ourselves
on our way toward death.

God says:
there are no sexes;

& still we amuse ourselves
arguing about whether or not
She is male
or He

female.

What You Need to Be a Writer

for Ben Barber

After the college
reading,
the eager
students gather.

They ask me
what you need
to be a writer

& I, feeling flippant,
jaunty
(because
I am wearing
an 18th century dress
& think
myself in love
again),
answer:

"Mazel,
determination,
talent,
& true
grit."

I even
believe it——

looking
as I do
like an
advertisement
for easy
success——

designer dress,
sly smile
on my lips
& silver boots
from
Oz.

Suppose
they saw me
my eyes
swollen
like sponges,
my hand
shaking
with betrayal,

my fear
rampant
in the dark?

Suppose they saw
the fear
of never
writing,
the fear
of being
alone,
the money fear,

the fear fear,
the fear
of succumbing
to fear?

& then
there's all
I did
not say:

to be
a writer
what you need
is

something
to say:

something
that burns
like a hot coal
in your gut

something
that pounds
like a pump
in your groin

& the courage
to love
like a wound

that never
heals.

Letter to My Lover After Seven Years

You gave me the child
that seamed my belly
& stitched up my life.

You gave me: one book of love poems,
five years of peace
& two of pain.

You gave me darkness, light, laughter
& the certain knowledge
that we someday die.

You gave me seven years
during which the cells of my body
died & were reborn.

Now we have died
into the limbo of lost loves,
that wreckage of memories
tarnishing with time,
that litany of losses
which grows longer with the years,
as more of our friends
descend underground
& the list of our loved dead
outstrips the list of the living.

Knowing as we do
our certain doom,
knowing as we do
the rarity of the gifts we gave
& received,
can we redeem
our love from the limbo,
dust it off like a fine sea trunk
found in an attic
& now more valuable
for its age & rarity
than a shining new one?

Probably not.
This page is spattered
with tears that streak the words
lose, losses, limbo.

I stand on a ledge in hell
still howling for our love.

If You Come Back

If you come back
now
before the roadblocks
are too many,
before too many bodies
are stacked
between us,
before the demilitarized zone
fills up with the mud
of betrayal,
& counter-betrayal,
we may still find
it in our hearts
to trust each other.
We may still find
it in our bodies
to fit together.
We may still find
that our minds
curl around the same
jokes and rejoice
in the same
hijinks.

But if we wait
till the bodies pile up
to the sky,
till the blood

dries in the muddy trench,
we may just find
that it turns
to pale powder
& blows away.

For we know that
love can dry up
as surely as arroyos
were once raging rivers,
as surely as swamps
are deserts now,
as surely as oceans
turn to sand.

I do not fear
the blood
as much as I fear
its drying
until the smallest breath
can blow
our love, our dreams,
our mingled flesh

away.

There Is Only One Story

There is only one story:
he loved her,
then stopped loving her,
while she did not
stop loving him.

There is only one story:
she loved him,
then stopped loving him,
while he did not
stop loving her.

The truth is simple:
you do not die
from love.

You only wish
you did.

My Love Is Too Much

My love is too much—
it embarrasses you—
blood, poems, babies,
red needs that telephone
from foreign countries,
black needs that spatter
the pages
of your white papery heart.

You would rather have a girl
with simpler needs:
lunch, sex, undemanding
loving,
dinner, wine, bed,
the occasional blow-job
& needs that are never
red as gaping wounds
but cool & blue
as television screens
in tract houses.

Oh my love,
those simple girls
with simple needs
read my books too.

They tell me they feel
the same as I do.

They tell me I transcribe
the language of their hearts.
They tell me I translate
their mute, unspoken pain
in the white light
of language.

Oh love,
no love
is ever wholly undemanding.
It can pretend coolness
until the pain comes,
until the first baby comes,
howling her own infant need
into a universe
that never summoned her.

The love you seek
cannot be found
except in the white pages
of recipe books.

It is cooking you seek,
not love,
cooking with sex coming after,
cool sex
that speaks to the penis alone,
& not the howling chaos
of the heart.

For Molly, Concerning God

Is God the one who eats the meat off the bones of dead people?

——Molly Miranda Jong-Fast, age 3½

God is the one,
Molly,
whether we call him
Him
or Her,
treeform or spewing
volcano,
Vesuvius or vulva,
penis-rock,
or reindeer-on-cave-wall,
God is the one
who eats
our meat,
Molly,
& we yield
our meat
up willingly.

Meat is our
element,
meat is our
lesson.

When our bodies fill
with each other,
when our blood swells
in our organs
aching for another,
body of meat,
heart of meat,
soul of meat,
we are only doing
what God wants
us to—
meat joining meat
to become insubstantial air,
meat fusing
with meat
to make
a small wonder
like you.

The wonder of you
is that you push
our questions
along into
the future—
so that I know
again
the wonder of meat
through you,
the wonder of meat
turning to philosophy,
the wonder of meat
transubstantiated
into poetry,
the wonder of
sky-blue meat
in your roundest eyes,
the wonder of
dawn-colored meat

in your cheeks & palms,
the wonder of meat
becoming
air.

You
are my theorem,
my proof,
my meaty metaphysics,
my little questioner,
my small Socrates
of the nursery-schoolyard.

To think that
such wonder
can come from meat!

Well then,
if God is hungry—
let Him eat,
let Her eat.

Poem for Molly's Fortieth Birthday

"Why do you
have stripes
in your forehead,
Mama?
Are you
old?"

Not old.
But not so
young
that I cannot
see
the world contracting
upon itself
& the circle
closing at the end.

As the furrows
in my brow
deepen,
I can see
myself
sinking back
into that childhood
street
I walked along
with my grandfather,
thinking *he* was old

at sixty-three
since I was four,
as you are four
to my
forty.

Forty years
to take
the road out.
Will another forty
take me
back?

Back to the street
I grew up on,
back to
my mother's breast,
back to the second
world war
of a second
child,
back
to the cradle
endlessly
rocking?

I am young
as *you* are,
Molly—
yet with stripes
in my brow;
I earn my youth
as you must earn
your age.

These stripes
are decorations
for my valor—

forty years
of marching
to a war
i could not declare,
nor locate,
yet have somehow
won.

Now,
I begin
to unwin,
unravelling
the sleeves
of care
that have
stitched up
this brow,
unravelling
the threads
that have kept
me scared,
as I pranced
over the world,
seemingly fearless,
working
without a net,
knowing
if I fell
it would
only be
into that same
childhood street,
where I dreaded
to tread
on the lines—
not knowing
the lines
would someday

tread
on me.

Molly,
when you are forty,
read this poem
& tell me:
have we won
or lost
the war?

The Horse from Hell

(Elegy for my grandfather who painted the sea & horses)

A dream of fantastic horses
galloping out of the sea,
the sea itself a dream,
a dream of green on green,
an age of indolence
where one-celled animals
blossom, once more, into limbs,
brains, pounding hooves,
out of the terrible innocence
of the waves.

Venice on the crest
of hell's typhoon,
sunami of my dreams
when, all at once,
I wake at three a.m.
in a tidal wave of love & sleeplessness,
anxiety & dread.

Up from the dream,
up on the shining white ledge of dread—
I dredge the deep
for proof that we do not die,
for proof that love

is a seawall against despair,
& find only
the one-celled dreams
dividing & dividing
as in the primal light.

O my grandfather,
you who painted the sea
so obsessively,
you who painted horses
galloping, galloping
out of the sea——
go now,
ride on the bare back
of the unsaddled,
unsaddleable horse
who would take you
straight to hell.

Gallop on the back
of all my nightmares;
dance in the foam
in a riot of hooves
& let the devil paint you
with his sea-green brush;
let him take you
into the waves at last,
until you fall,
chiming forever,
through the seaweed bells,
lost like the horses of San Marco,
but not for good.

Down through the hulls
of gelatinous fish,
down through the foamless foam
which coats your bones,
down through the undersea green

which changes your flesh
into pure pigment,
grinding your eyes down
to the essential cobalt blue.
Let the bones of my poems
support what is left of you—
ashes & nightmares,
canvasses half-finished & fading worksheets.

O my grandfather,
as you die,
a poem forms on my lips,
as foam forms
on the ocean's morning mouth,
& I sing in honor of the sea & you—

the sea who defies all paintings
& all poems
& you
who defy
the sea.

States